13.b
1756

D0982058

COUNTERFEIT GODS

COUNTERFEIT GODS

*The Empty Promises of Money,
Sex, and Power, and the
Only Hope that Matters*

TIMOTHY KELLER

DUTTON

DUTTON
Published by Penguin Group (U.S.A) Inc.
375 Hudson Street, New York, New York 10014, U.S.A.
Penguin Group (Canada), 90 Eglinton Avenue East, Suite 700, Toronto, Ontario M4P 2Y3, Canada (a division of Pearson Penguin Canada Inc.); Penguin Books Ltd, 80 Strand, London WC2R 0RL, England; Penguin Ireland, 25 St Stephen's Green, Dublin 2, Ireland (a division of Penguin Books Ltd); Penguin Group (Australia), 250 Camberwell Road, Camberwell, Victoria 3124, Australia (a division of Pearson Australia Group Pty Ltd); Penguin Books India Pvt Ltd, 11 Community Centre, Panchsheel Park, New Delhi—110 017, India; Penguin Group (NZ), 67 Apollo Drive, Rosedale, North Shore 0632, New Zealand (a division of Pearson New Zealand Ltd); Penguin Books (South Africa) (Pty) Ltd, 24 Sturdee Avenue, Rosebank, Johannesburg 2196, South Africa

Penguin Books Ltd, Registered Offices: 80 Strand, London WC2R 0RL, England

Published by Dutton, a member of Penguin Group (U.S.A) Inc.

First printing, October 2009
10   9   8   7   6

 REGISTERED TRADEMARK—MARCA REGISTRADA

LIBRARY OF CONGRESS CATALOGING-IN-PUBLICATION DATA

Keller, Timothy J., 1950–
Counterfeit gods : the empty promises of money, sex, and power, and the only hope that matters / Timothy Keller.
p.   cm.
ISBN 978-0-525-95136-0 (hardcover)
1. Idolatry.   2. Christian life—Presbyterian authors.   I. Title.
BV4627.I34K45   2009
241'.3—dc22   2009028142

Printed in the United States of America
Set in ITC Galliard
Designed by Leonard Telesca

To my sons,
David, Michael, and Jonathan,
who can detect the counterfeit

Contents

Contents

INTRODUCTION
THE IDOL FACTORY

There are more idols in the world than there are realities.
—Friedrich Nietzsche, *Twilight of the Idols*

A Strange Melancholy

After the global economic crisis began in mid-2008, there followed a tragic string of suicides of formerly wealthy and well-connected individuals. The acting chief financial officer of Freddie Mac, the Federal Home Loan Mortgage Corporation, hanged himself in his basement. The chief executive of Sheldon Good, a leading U.S. real estate auction firm, shot himself in the head behind the wheel of his red Jaguar. A French money manager who invested the wealth of many of Europe's royal and leading families, and who had lost $1.4 billion of his clients' money in Bernard Madoff's Ponzi scheme, slit his wrists and died in his

Madison Avenue office. A Danish senior executive with HSBC Bank hanged himself in the wardrobe of his £500-a-night suite in Knightsbridge, London. When a Bear Stearns executive learned that he would not be hired by JPMorgan Chase, which had bought his collapsed firm, he took a drug overdose and leapt from the twenty-ninth floor of his office building. A friend said, "This Bear Stearns thing . . . broke his spirit."[1] It was grimly reminiscent of the suicides in the wake of the 1929 stock market crash.

In the 1830s, when Alexis de Tocqueville recorded his famous observations on America, he noted a "strange melancholy that haunts the inhabitants . . . in the midst of abundance."[2] Americans believed that prosperity could quench their yearning for happiness, but such a hope was illusory, because, de Tocqueville added, "the incomplete joys of this world will never satisfy [the human] heart."[3] This strange melancholy manifests itself in many ways, but always leads to the same despair of not finding what is sought.

There is a difference between sorrow and despair. Sorrow is pain for which there are sources of consolation. Sorrow comes from losing one good thing among others, so that, if you experience a career reversal, you can find comfort in your family to get you through it. Despair, however, is inconsolable, because it comes from losing an *ultimate* thing. When you lose the ultimate source of your meaning or hope, there are no alternative sources to turn to. It breaks your spirit.

What is the cause of this "strange melancholy" that permeates our society even during boom times of frenetic activity, and which turns to outright despair when prosperity diminishes? De Tocqueville says it comes from taking some "incomplete joy of this world" and building your entire life on it. That is the definition of idolatry.

A Culture Filled with Idols

To contemporary people the word *idolatry* conjures up pictures of primitive people bowing down before statues. The biblical book of Acts in the New Testament contains vivid descriptions of the cultures of the ancient Greco-Roman world. Each city worshipped its favorite deities and built shrines around their images for worship. When Paul went to Athens he saw that it was literally filled with images of these divinities (Acts 17:16). The Parthenon of Athena overshadowed everything, but other deities were represented in every public space. There was Aphrodite, the goddess of beauty; Ares, the god of war; Artemis, the goddess of fertility and wealth; Hephaestus, the god of craftsmanship.

Our contemporary society is not fundamentally different from these ancient ones. Each culture is dominated by its own set of idols. Each has its "priesthoods," its totems and rituals. Each one has its shrines—whether office towers, spas and gyms, studios, or stadiums—where sacrifices must be made in order to procure the blessings of the good life and ward off disaster. What are the gods of beauty, power, money, and achievement but these same things that have assumed mythic proportions in our individual lives and in our society? We may not physically kneel before the statue of Aphrodite, but many young women today are driven into depression and eating disorders by an obsessive concern over their body image. We may not actually burn incense to Artemis, but when money and career are raised to cosmic proportions, we perform a kind of child sacrifice, neglecting family and community to achieve a higher place in business and gain more wealth and prestige.

After New York's governor Eliot Spitzer destroyed his career because of his involvement in a high-priced prostitution ring, David Brooks noted how our culture has produced a class of high achievers with "rank-link imbalances." They have social skills for vertical relationships, for improving their rank with mentors and bosses, but none for genuine bonding in horizontal relationships with spouses, friends, and family. "Countless presidential candidates say they are running on behalf of their families, even though their entire lives have been spent on the campaign trail away from their families." As the years go by they come to the sickening realization that "their grandeur is not enough and that they are lonely."[4] Many of their children and spouses are alienated from them. They seek to heal the hurt. They get into affairs or take other desperate measures to medicate the inner emptiness. Then comes family breakdown or scandal or both.

They had sacrificed everything to the god of success, but it wasn't enough. In ancient times, the deities were bloodthirsty and hard to appease. They still are.

Idols of the Heart

It would have been hard to make this case convincingly during the era of the dot-com boom and of the real estate and stock bubble of the last twenty years. However, the great economic meltdown of 2008–2009 has laid bare what is now being called "the culture of greed." Long ago, Saint Paul wrote that greed was not just bad behavior. "Greed is idolatry," he wrote. (Colossians 3:5) Money, he advised, can take on divine attributes, and our relationship to it then approximates worship and obeisance.

Money can become a spiritual addiction, and like all addictions it hides its true proportions from its victims. We take more and greater risks to get an ever diminishing satisfaction from the thing we crave, until a breakdown occurs. When we begin to recover, we ask, "What were we thinking? How could we have been so blind?" We wake up like people with a hangover who can hardly remember the night before. But why? Why did we act so irrationally? Why did we completely lose sight of what is right?

The Bible's answer is that the human heart is an "idol factory."[5]

When most people think of "idols" they have in mind literal statues—or the next pop star anointed by Simon Cowell. Yet while traditional idol worship still occurs in many places of the world, internal idol worship, within the heart, is universal. In Ezekiel 14:3, God says about elders of Israel, "These men have set up their idols in their *hearts.*" Like us, the elders must have responded to this charge, "Idols? What idols? I don't see any idols." God was saying that the human heart takes good things like a successful career, love, material possessions, even family, and turns them into ultimate things. Our hearts deify them as the center of our lives, because, we think, they can give us significance and security, safety and fulfillment, if we attain them.[6]

The central plot device of *The Lord of the Rings* is the Dark Lord Sauron's Ring of Power, which corrupts anyone who tries to use it, however good his or her intentions. The Ring is what Professor Tom Shippey calls "a psychic amplifier," which takes the heart's fondest desires and magnifies them to idolatrous proportions.[7] Some good characters in the book want to liberate slaves, or preserve their people's land, or visit wrongdoers with just punishment. These are all good objectives. But the Ring makes them willing to do *any*thing to achieve them, anything at all. It turns the good thing into an absolute that overturns every other allegiance or value. The wearer of the Ring becomes increasingly enslaved and addicted to it, for an idol is something we cannot live without. We must have it, and therefore it drives us to break rules we once honored, to harm others and even ourselves in order to get it. Idols are spiritual addictions that lead to terrible evil, in Tolkien's novel and real life.

Anything Can Be an Idol

Cultural moments like the one we are in provide us with an opportunity. Many people are now more open to the Bible's warning that money can become much more than money. It can become a powerful life-altering, culture-shaping god, an idol that breaks the hearts of its worshippers. The bad news is that we are so fixated on the problem of greed, which we tend to see in "those rich people over there," that we don't realize the most fundamental truth. Anything can be an idol, and everything has been an idol.

The most famous moral code in the world is the Decalogue, the Ten Commandments. The very first commandment is "I am the Lord your God . . . you shall have no other gods before me" (Exodus 20:3). That leads to the natural question—"What do you mean, 'other gods'?" An answer comes immediately. "You shall not make for yourself an idol in the form of anything in heaven above or on the earth beneath or in the waters below. You shall not bow down to them or worship them. . . ." (Exodus 20:4–5) That includes everything in the world! Most people know you can make a god out of money. Most know you can make god out of sex. However, *any*thing in life can serve as an idol, a God-alternative, a counterfeit god.

I recently heard the account of a field army officer who so exorbitantly pursued physical and military discipline with his troops that he broke their morale. That led to a communication breakdown during combat that resulted in fatalities. I knew a woman who had experienced periods of poverty as she grew up. As an adult she was so eager for financial security that she passed over many good prospective relationships in order to marry a wealthy man she did not really love. This led to an early divorce and to all the economic struggles she feared so much. It appears that some major league baseball players, in a quest to play not just well but at a Hall of Fame level, took steroids and other drugs. As a result, their bodies are more broken and their reputations more sullied than if they had been willing to be good rather than great. The very things upon which these people were building all their happiness turned to dust in their hands *because* they had built all their happiness upon them. In each case, a good thing among many was turned into a supreme thing, so that its demands overrode all competing values.[8] But counterfeit gods always disappoint, and often destructively so.

Is it wrong to want disciplined troops, or financial security, or athletic prowess? Not at all. But these stories point to a common mistake people make when they hear about the biblical concept of idolatry. We think that idols are bad things, but that is almost never the case. The greater the good, the more likely we are to expect that it can satisfy our deepest needs and hopes. Anything can serve as a counterfeit god, especially the very best things in life.

How to Make a God

What is an idol? It is anything more important to you than God, anything that absorbs your heart and imagination more than God, anything you seek to give you what only God can give.[9]

A counterfeit god is anything so central and essential to your life that, should you lose it, your life would feel hardly worth living. An idol has such a controlling position in your heart that you can spend most of your passion and energy, your emotional and financial resources, on it without a second thought. It can be family and children, or career and making money, or achievement and critical acclaim, or saving "face" and social standing. It can be a romantic relationship, peer approval, competence and skill, secure and comfortable circumstances, your beauty or your brains, a great political or social cause, your morality and virtue, or even success in the Christian ministry. When your meaning in life is to fix someone else's life, we may call it "co-dependency" but it is really idolatry. An idol is whatever you look at and say, in your heart of hearts, "If I have that, then I'll feel my life has meaning, then I'll know I have value, then I'll feel significant and secure." There are many ways to describe that kind of relationship to something, but perhaps the best one is *worship*.

The old pagans were not fanciful when they depicted virtually everything as a god. They had sex gods, work gods, war gods, money gods, nation gods—for the simple fact that anything can be a god that rules and serves as a deity in the heart of a person or in the life of a people. For example, physical beauty is a pleasant thing, but if you "deify" it, if you make it the most important thing in a person's life or a culture's life, then you have Aphrodite, not just beauty. You have people, and an entire culture, constantly agonizing over appearance, spending inordinate amounts of time and money on it, and foolishly evaluating character on the basis of it. If anything becomes more fundamental than God to your happiness, meaning in life, and identity, then it is an idol.

The biblical concept of idolatry is an extremely sophisticated idea, integrating intellectual, psychological, social, cultural, and spiritual categories. There are personal idols, such as romantic love and family; or money, power, and achievement; or access to particular social circles; or the emotional dependence of others on you; or health, fitness, and physical beauty. Many look to these things for the hope, meaning, and fulfillment that only God can provide.

There are cultural idols, such as military power, technological progress, and economic prosperity. The idols of traditional societies include family, hard work, duty, and moral virtue, while those of Western cultures are individual freedom, self-discovery, personal affluence, and fulfillment. All these good things can and do take on disproportionate size and power within a society. They promise us safety, peace, and happiness if only we base our lives on them.

There can also be intellectual idols, often called

ideologies. For example, European intellectuals in the late nineteenth and early twentieth centuries became largely convinced of Rousseau's view of the innate goodness of human nature, that all of our social problems were the result of poor education and socialization. World War II shattered this illusion. Beatrice Webb, whom many consider the architect of Britain's modern welfare state, wrote:

> Somewhere in my diary—1890?—I wrote "I have staked all on the essential goodness of human nature. . . ." [Now thirty-five years later I realize] how permanent are the evil impulses and instincts in man—how little you can count on changing some of these—for instance the appeal of wealth and power—by any change in the [social] machinery. . . . No amount of knowledge or science will be of any avail unless we can curb the bad impulse.[10]

In 1920, in his book *Outline of History,* H. G. Wells praised belief in human progress. In 1933, in *The Shape of Things to Come,* appalled by the selfishness and violence of European nations, Wells believed the only hope was for intellectuals to seize control and run a compulsory educational program stressing peace and justice and equity. In 1945, in *A Mind at the End of Its Tether,* he wrote, "*Homo sapiens,* as he has been pleased to call himself, is . . . played out." What happened to Wells and Webb? They had taken a partial truth and made it into an all-encompassing truth, by which everything could be explained and improved. To "stake everything" on human goodness was to put it in the place of God.

There are also idols, nonnegotiable absolute values, in every vocational field. In the business world, self-expression is suppressed for the ultimate value, profit. In the art world, however, it is the other way around. Everything is sacrificed to self-expression, and it is done in the name of redemption. This, it is thought, is what the human race needs above all. There are idols everywhere.

Love, Trust, and Obey

The Bible uses three basic metaphors to describe how people relate to the idols of their hearts. They *love* idols, *trust* idols, and *obey* idols.[11]

The Bible sometimes speaks of idols using a marital metaphor. God should be our true Spouse, but when we desire and delight in other things more than God we commit spiritual adultery.[12] Romance or success can become "false lovers" that promise to make us feel loved and valued. Idols capture our imagination, and we can locate them by looking at our daydreams. What do we enjoy imagining? What are our fondest dreams? We look to our idols to love us, to provide us with value and a sense of beauty, significance, and worth.

The Bible often speaks of idols using the religious metaphor. God should be our true Savior, but we look to personal achievement or financial prosperity to give us the peace and security we need.[13] Idols give us a sense of being in control, and we can locate them by looking at our nightmares. What do we fear the most? What, if we lost it, would make life not worth living? We make "sacrifices" to appease and please our gods, who we believe will protect us. We look to our idols to provide us with a sense of confidence and safety.

The Bible also speaks of idols using a political metaphor. God should be our only Lord and Master, but whatever we love and trust we also serve. Anything that becomes more important and nonnegotiable to us than God becomes an enslaving idol.[14] In this paradigm, we can locate idols by looking at our most unyielding emotions. What makes us uncontrollably angry, anxious, or despondent? What racks us with a guilt we can't shake? Idols control us, since we feel we must have them or life is meaningless.

Whatever controls us is our lord. The person who seeks power is controlled by power. The person who seeks acceptance is controlled by the people he or she wants to please. We do not control ourselves. We are controlled by the lord of our lives.[15]

What many people call "psychological problems" are simple issues of idolatry. Perfectionism, workaholism, chronic indecisiveness, the need to control the lives of others—all of these stem from making good things into idols that then drive us into the ground as we try to appease them. Idols dominate our lives.

The Opportunity of Disenchantment

As we have seen, there is a big difference between sorrow and despair, since despair is unbearable sorrow. In most cases, the difference between the two is idolatry. A Korean businessman killed himself after losing most of a $370 million investment. "When the nation's stock market index fell below 1,000, he stopped eating and went on a drinking binge for days and finally decided to kill himself," his wife told police.[16] In the midst of the great financial crisis of 2008–2009 I heard a man named Bill recount that three years before he had become a Christian and his ultimate security had shifted from money to his relationship with God through Christ.[17] "If this economic meltdown had happened more than three years ago, well, I don't know how I could have faced it, how I would have even kept going. Today, I can tell you honestly, I've never been happier in my life."

Though we think we live in a secular world, idols, the glittering gods of our age, hold title to the functional trust of our hearts. With the global economy in shambles, many of those idols that we have worshipped for years have come crashing down around us. This is a great opportunity. We are briefly experiencing "disenchantment." In the old stories, that meant that the spell cast by the evil sorcerer was broken and there was the chance to escape. Such times come to us as individuals, when some great enterprise, pursuit, or person on which we have built our hopes fails to deliver what (we thought) was promised. It very rarely comes to an entire society.

The way forward, out of despair, is to discern the idols of our hearts and our culture. But that will not be enough. The only way to free ourselves from the destructive influence of counterfeit gods is to turn back to the true one. The living God, who revealed himself both at Mount Sinai and on the Cross, is the only Lord who, if you find him, can truly fulfill you, and, if you fail him, can truly forgive you.

COUNTERFEIT GODS

ONE

❧❧❧❧

All You've Ever Wanted

The Worst Thing that Can Happen

Most people spend their lives trying to make their heart's fondest dreams come true. Isn't that what life is all about, "the pursuit of happiness"? We search endlessly for ways to acquire the things we desire, and we are willing to sacrifice much to achieve them. We never imagine that getting our heart's deepest desires might be the worst thing that can ever happen to us.

My wife and I once knew a single woman, Anna, who wanted desperately to have children. She eventually married, and contrary to the expectations of her doctors, was able to bear two healthy children despite her age. But her dreams did not come true. Her overpowering drive to give her children a perfect life made it impossible for her to actually enjoy them. Her overprotectiveness, fears and anxieties, and her need to control every detail of her children's lives made the family miserable. Anna's oldest child did poorly in school and showed signs of serious emotional problems. The younger child was filled with anger. There's a good chance her drive to give her children wonderful lives will actually be the thing that ruins them. Getting her heart's deepest desire may end up being the worst thing that ever happened to her.

In the late 1980s, Cynthia Heimel wrote, "The minute a person becomes a celebrity is the same minute he/she becomes a monster," and then gave the names of three well-known Hollywood stars she had known before they became famous. They had been "once perfectly pleasant human beings . . . now they have become supreme beings and their wrath is awful." She went on to say that under the pressure of fame and celebrity all your character flaws and miseries become twice as bad as they were before.[18] You might be curious who these 1980s stars were, but you don't need to know that. Right now, there are any number of "bold-face names" living out the same patterns on the front pages of the newspapers. The names change but the pattern is permanent.

The Inevitability of Idolatry

Why is getting your heart's deepest desire so often a disaster? In the book of Romans, Saint Paul wrote that one of the worst things God can do to someone is to "give them over to the desires of their hearts" (Romans 1:24). Why would the greatest punishment imaginable be to allow someone to achieve their fondest dream? It is because our hearts fashion these desires into idols. In that same chapter, Paul summarized the history of the human race in one sentence: "They worshipped and served created things rather than the Creator" (Romans 1:25). Every human being must live for something. Something must capture our imaginations, our heart's most fundamental allegiance and hope. But, the Bible tells us, without the intervention of the Holy Spirit, that object will never be God himself.

If we look to some created thing to give us the meaning, hope, and happiness that only God himself can give, it will eventually fail to deliver and break our hearts. The woman, Anna, who was ruining her children's lives did not "love her children too much," but rather loved God too little in relationship to them. As a result, her child-gods were crushed under the weight of her expectations.

Two Jewish philosophers who knew the Scriptures intimately concluded: "The central . . . principle of the Bible [is] the rejection of idolatry."[19] The Bible is therefore filled with story after story depicting the innumerable forms and devastating effects of idol worship. Every counterfeit god a heart can choose—whether love, money, success, or power—has a powerful biblical narrative that explains how that particular kind of idolatry works itself out in our lives.

One of the central figures of the Bible is Abraham. Like most men in ancient times, he longed for a son and heir who would carry on his name. In Abraham's case, however, that desire had become the deepest desire of his heart. Finally, beyond all hope, a son was born to him. He now had all he had ever wanted. Then God asked him to give it all up.

The Call of Abraham

According to the Bible, God came to Abraham and made him a staggering promise. If he would obey him faithfully, God would bless all the nations of the earth through him and his descendents. For this to happen, however, Abraham had to *go*. "Leave your country, your people, and your father's house, and go to the land that I will show you" (Genesis 12:1–3). God called Abraham to leave all that was familiar—his friends, most of his family, and everything that he believed meant safety, prosperity, and peace—and go out into the wilderness, uncertain of his destination. He was asked to give up, for God's sake, nearly all the worldly hopes and things that a human heart desires.

And he did. He was called to "go" and he went, "though he did not know where he was going" (Hebrews 11:8).

However, while God's call had demanded that he give up his other hopes, it had also given him a new one. The prophecy was that the nations of the earth would be blessed through his family, "your offspring" (Genesis 12:7). That meant he had to have children. Sarah, Abraham's wife, had been unable to conceive. Biologically speaking, having children seemed impossible. But God promised that Abraham would have a son.

As the years turned into decades, however, the divine promise became more and more difficult to believe. Finally, after Abraham was over a hundred years old, and Sarah over the age of ninety (Genesis 17:17, 21:5), she gave birth to a son, Isaac. This was clearly divine intervention, and so Isaac's name meant "laughter," a reference to both his parents' joy and to their difficulty in believing that God would ever give them what he had promised.

The years of agonized waiting had taken their toll, as any couple struggling with infertility can attest. The nearly endless delays refined Abraham's faith, which was crucially important. However, the years of infertility had also had another effect. No man had ever longed for a son more than Abraham. He had given up everything else to wait for this. When his son came, he felt, then his community would finally see he hadn't been a fool to give up everything to trust God's word. Then he would finally have an heir, a son in his own likeness, the thing all ancient Middle Eastern patriarchs wanted. He had waited and sacrificed, and finally his wife had a baby and it was a boy!

But the question now was—had he been waiting and sacrificing for God, or for the boy? Was God just a means to an end? To whom was Abraham ultimately giving his heart? Did Abraham have the peace, humility, boldness, and unmovable poise that come to those who trust in God rather than in circumstances, public opinion, or their own competence? Had he learned to trust God *alone,* to love God for himself, not just for what he could get out of God? No, not yet.

The Second Call of Abraham

When our friend Anna, the woman who had longed for children, at last became pregnant, she thought that she would live "happily ever after." Sadly, that did not happen, and it rarely does. Many couples longing for a child believe that having a child will solve all their problems, but that is never the case. Readers of Genesis 12–21 might likewise think that the birth of Isaac would have been the climax and last chapter of Abraham's life. His faith had triumphed. Now he could die a happy man, having fulfilled God's call to him to leave his homeland and wait for a son to be born. But then, to our surprise, Abraham got another call from God. And it could not have been more shocking.

> *Take your son, your only son, Isaac, whom you love, and go to the region of Moriah. Sacrifice him there as a burnt offering on one of the mountains I will tell you about.*

Genesis 22:2

This was the ultimate test. Isaac was now *everything* to Abraham, as God's call makes clear. He does not refer to the boy as "Isaac," but as "your son, your only son, whom you love." Abraham's affection had become adoration. Previously, Abraham's meaning in life had been dependent on God's word. Now it was becoming dependent on Isaac's love and well-being. The center of Abraham's life was shifting. God was not saying you cannot love your son, but that you must not turn a loved one into a counterfeit god. If anyone puts a child in the place of the true God, it creates an idolatrous love that will smother the child and strangle the relationship.

The Horror of the Command

Many readers over the years have had understandable objections to this story. They have interpreted the "moral" of this story as meaning that doing cruel and violent things is fine, as long as you believe it is God's will. No one has spoken more vividly about this than Søren Kierkegaard, whose book *Fear and Trembling* is based on the story of Abraham and Isaac. Kierkegaard ultimately reasons that faith is irrational and absurd. Abraham thought the command made no sense at all, and contradicted everything else God had ever said, yet he followed the command.

Would this command have been totally irrational to Abraham? Kierkegaard's interpretation of the story does not take into consideration the meaning of the firstborn son in Jewish thought and symbolism. Jon Levenson, a Jewish scholar who teaches at Harvard, has written *The Death and Resurrection of the Beloved Son*. In this volume he reminds us that ancient cultures were not as individualistic as ours. People's hopes and dreams were never for their own personal success, prosperity, or prominence. Since everyone was part of a family, and no one lived apart from the family, these things were only sought for the entire clan. We must also remember the ancient law of primogeniture. The oldest son got the majority of the estate and wealth so the family would not lose its place in society.[20]

In an individualistic culture like ours, an adult's identity and sense of worth is often bound up in abilities and achievements, but in ancient times, all the hopes and dreams of a man and his family rested in the firstborn son.[21] The call to give up the firstborn son would be analogous to a surgeon giving up the use of his hands, or of a visual artist losing the use of her eyes.

Levenson argues that we can only understand God's command to Abraham against this cultural background. The Bible repeatedly states that, because of the Israelites' sinfulness, the lives of their firstborn are automatically forfeit, though they might be redeemed through regular sacrifice (Exodus 22:29, 34:20) or through service at the tabernacle among the Levites (Numbers 3:40–41) or through a ransom payment to the tabernacle and priests (Numbers 3:46–48). When God brought judgment on Egypt for enslaving the Israelites, his ultimate punishment was taking the lives of their firstborn. Their firstborns' lives were forfeit, because of the sins of the families and the nation. Why? The firstborn son *was* the family. So when God told the Israelites that the firstborn's life belonged to him unless ransomed, he was saying in the most vivid way possible in those cultures that every family on earth owed a debt to eternal justice—the debt of sin.

All this is crucial for interpreting God's directive to Abraham. If Abraham had heard a voice sounding like God's saying, "Get up and kill Sarah," Abraham would probably never have done it. He would have rightly assumed that he was hallucinating, for God would not ask him to do something that clearly contradicted everything he had ever said about justice and righteousness. But when God stated that his only son's life was forfeit, that was *not* an irrational, contradictory statement to him. Notice, God was not asking him to walk over into Isaac's tent and just murder him. He asked him to make him a burnt offering. He was calling in Abraham's debt. His son was going to die for the sins of the family.

The Walk into the Mountains

Though the command was comprehensible, that did not make it any less terrible. Abraham was faced with the ultimate question: "God is holy. Our sin means that Isaac's life is forfeit. Yet God is also a God of grace. He has said he wants to bless the world through Isaac. How can God be both holy and just and still graciously fulfill his promise of salvation?" Abraham did not know. But he went. He acted in line with another figure in the Old Testament, Job, who was sent countless afflictions with no explanation. Job, however, says about the Lord, "He knows what he is doing with me, and when he has tested me, I will come forth as pure gold" (Job 23:10).[22]

How did Abraham get himself to walk up into the mountains in obedience to God's call? The masterful Hebrew narrative gives us tantalizing hints. He told his servants that "*we* will come back to you" (Genesis 22:5). It is unlikely he had any specific idea of what God would do. But he did not go up the mountain saying, "I *can* do it," filled with willpower and self-talk. Rather, he went up saying, "God will do it . . . but I don't know how." Do what? God would somehow remove the debt on the firstborn and still keep the promise of grace.

Abraham was not just exercising "blind faith." He was not saying, "This is crazy, this is murder, but I'm going to do it anyway." Instead he was saying, "I know God is *both* holy *and* gracious. I don't know how he is going to be both—but I know he will." If he had not believed that he was in debt to a holy God, he would have been too angry to go. But if he had not also believed that God was a God of grace, he would have been too crushed and hopeless to go. He would have just lain down and died. It was only because he knew

God was both holy and loving that he was able to put one foot after another up that mountain.

Finally Abraham and his son could see the sacrifice site.

> *When they reached the place God had told him about, Abraham built an altar there and arranged the wood on it. He bound his son Isaac and laid him on the altar on top of the wood. Then he reached out his hand and took the knife to slay his son.*
>
> Genesis 22:9–10

But at that very moment, the voice of God came to him from heaven, "Abraham! Abraham!"

"Here I am," he replied from the precipice.

"Do not lay a hand on the boy . . . for now I know that you fear God, because you have not withheld from me your son, your only son" (Verse 12). And at that moment Abraham saw a ram caught by its horns in a thicket. Abraham untied Isaac and sacrificed it in place of his son.

The Danger of the Best Things in the World

What was this incident all about? It was about two things, one that Abraham probably saw fairly well, and one that he could not have understood clearly.

What Abraham was able to see was that this test was about loving God supremely. In the end the Lord said to him, "Now I know you fear God." In the Bible, this does not refer so much to being "afraid" of God as to being wholeheartedly committed to him. In Psalm 130:4, for example, we see that "the fear of God" is increased by an experience of God's grace and forgiveness. What it describes is a loving, joyful awe and wonder before the greatness of God. The Lord is saying, "Now I know that you love me more than anything in the world." That's what "the fear of God" means.

This doesn't mean that God was trying to find out if Abraham loved him. The All-seeing God knows the state of every heart. Rather, God was putting Abraham through the furnace, so his love for God could finally "come forth as pure gold." It is not hard to see why God was using Isaac as the means for this. If God had not intervened, Abraham would have certainly come to love his son more than anything in the world, if he did not already do so. That would have been idolatry, and all idolatry is destructive.

From this perspective we see that God's extremely rough treatment of Abraham was actually merciful. Isaac was a wonderful gift to Abraham, but he was not safe to have and hold until Abraham was willing to put God first. As long as Abraham never had to choose between his son and obedience to God, he could not see that his love was becoming idolatrous. In a similar way, we may not realize how idolatrous our career has become to us, until we are faced with a situation in which telling the truth or acting with integrity would mean a serious blow to our professional advancement. If we are not willing to hurt our career in order to do God's will, our job will become a counterfeit god.

How could the woman we met earlier in this chapter, Anna, have given God what he asked of Abraham? Counselors would tell her she has to stop pushing her children into activities and projects they have no aptitude for. She has to stop punishing them emotionally for bad grades. She would have to give them the freedom to fail. That's all true, but there is an underlying issue that has to be confronted. She must be able to say in her heart, "My desire for completely successful and happy children is selfish. It's all about my need to feel worthwhile and valuable. If I really knew God's love— then I could accept less-than-perfect kids and wouldn't be crushing them. If God's love meant more to me than my children, I could love my children less selfishly and more truly." Anna has to put her "Isaacs" on the altar and give God the central place in her life.

Her overcontrol of her children was not only an unwillingness to let God be God in her own life, but also in their lives. Anna could not imagine that God might have a plan for her children's lives wiser than her own.

She had mapped out a perfect life, without failures or disappointments. But that *is* more of a flawed life-plan than the bumpy ride God inevitably maps out for us. People who have never suffered in life have less empathy for others, little knowledge of their own shortcomings and limitations, no endurance in the face of hardship, and unrealistic expectations for life. As the New Testament book of Hebrews tells us, anyone God loves experiences hardship (Hebrews 12:1–8).

The success and love of Anna's children has been more important to her self-image than the glory and love of God. Though she believes in God with her mind, her heart's deepest satisfaction comes from hearing a child saying, "Oh, Mother, I owe everything to you!" Tragically, she may never hear the words that she longs for most, because her inordinate need for their approval is pushing away the ones she loves most. She must be willing to put God first, to trust God with her children by letting them fail, and to find her peace in his love and will. She needs to follow Abraham up into the mountains.

Abraham took that journey, and only after that could Abraham love Isaac well and wisely. If Isaac had become the main hope and joy of Abraham's life, his father would have either overdisciplined him (because he needed his son to be "perfect") or underdisciplined him (because he couldn't bear his son's displeasure) or both. He would have overindulged him but also become overly angry and cruel, perhaps even violent, when his son disappointed him. Why? Idols enslave. Isaac's love and success would have become Abraham's only identity and joy. He would have become inordinately angry, anxious, and depressed if Isaac ever failed to obey and love him. And fail he would have, since no child can bear the full weight of godhood. Abraham's expectations would have driven him away or twisted and disfigured his spirit.

Abraham's agonizing walk into the mountains was therefore the final stage of a long journey in which God was turning him from an average man into one of the greatest figures in history. The three great monotheistic faiths of the world today, Judaism, Islam, and Christianity, name Abraham as founder. Over one half the people in the human race consider him their spiritual father. That would have never happened unless God had dealt with the idol of Abraham's heart.

The Substitute

This famous incident was also about something that Abraham could not see, or at least not see very well in his time. Why had Isaac not been sacrificed? The sins of Abraham and his family were still there. How could a holy and just God overlook them? Well, a substitute was offered, a ram. But was it the ram's blood that took away the debt of the firstborn? No.

Many years later, in those same mountains,[23] another firstborn son was stretched out on the wood to die. But there on Mount Calvary, when the beloved son of God cried, "My God, my God—why hast thou forsaken me?" there was no voice from heaven announcing deliverance. Instead, God the Father paid the price in silence. Why? The true substitute for Abraham's son was God's only Son, Jesus, who died to bear our punishment. "For Christ died for sin once for all, the just for the unjust, to bring us to God" (1 Peter 3:18). Paul understood the true meaning of Isaac's story when he deliberately applied its language to Jesus: "He who did not spare his own Son, but gave him up for us all—how will he not also, along with him, freely give us all things?" (Romans 8:32)

Here, then, is the practical answer to our own idolatries, to the "Isaacs" in our lives, which are not spiritually safe to have and hold. We need to offer them up. We need to find a way to keep from clutching them too tightly, of being enslaved to them. We will never do so by mouthing abstractions about how great God is. We have to know, to be assured, that God so loves, cherishes, and delights in us that we can rest our hearts in him for our significance and security and handle anything that happens in life.

But how?

God saw Abraham's sacrifice and said, "Now I know that you love me, because you did not withhold your only son from me." But how much more can we look at *his* sacrifice on the Cross, and say to God, "Now, *we* know that you love *us*. For you did not withhold your son, your only son, whom you love, from us." When the magnitude of what he did dawns on us, it makes it possible finally to rest our hearts in him rather than in anything else.

Jesus alone makes sense of this story. The only way that God can be both "just" (demanding payment of our debt of sin) *and* "justifier"[24] (providing salvation and grace) is because years later another Father went up another "mount" called Calvary with his firstborn and offered him there for us all. You will never be as great, as secure in God, as courageous, as Abraham became simply by trying hard, but only by believing in the Savior to whom this event points. Only if Jesus lived and died for us can you have a God of infinite love and holiness at once. Then you can be absolutely sure he loves you.

Your Walk into the Mountains

Think of the many disappointments and troubles that beset us. Look at them more closely, and you will realize that the most agonizing of them have to do with our own "Isaacs." In our lives there are always some things that we invest in to get a level of joy and fulfillment that only God can give. The most painful times in our lives are times in which our Isaacs, our idols, are being threatened or removed. When that happens we can respond in two ways. We can opt for bitterness and despair. We will feel entitled to wallow in those feelings, saying, "I've worked all my life to get to this place in my career, and now it's all gone!" or "I've slaved my whole life to give that girl a good life, and this is how she repays me!" We may feel at liberty to lie, cheat, take revenge, or throw away our principles in order to get some relief. Or we may simply live in a permanent despondency.

Or else, like Abraham, you could take a walk up into the mountains. You could say, "I see that you may be calling me to live my life without something I never thought I could live without. But if I have you, I have the only wealth, health, love, honor, and security I really need and cannot lose." As many have learned and later taught, you don't realize Jesus is all you need until Jesus is all you have.

Many, if not most, of these counterfeit gods can remain in our lives once we have "demoted" them below God. Then they won't control us and bedevil us with anxiety, pride, anger, and drivenness. Nevertheless, we must not make the mistake of thinking that this story means all we have to do is be *willing* to part with our idols rather than actually leave them behind. If Abraham had gone up the mountain thinking, "All I'll have to do is put Isaac on the altar, not really give him up"— he would have failed the test! Something is safe for us to maintain in our lives only if it has really stopped being an idol. That can happen only when we are truly willing to live without it, when we truly say from the heart: "Because I have God, I can live without you."

Sometimes God seems to be killing us when he's actually saving us. Here he was turning Abraham into a great man—but on the outside it looked like God was being cruel. To follow God in such circumstances seems to some to be "blind faith," but actually it is vigorous, grateful faith. The Bible is filled with stories of figures such as Joseph, Moses, and David in which God seemed to have abandoned them, but later it is revealed he was dealing with the destructive idols in their lives and that could only have come to pass through their experience of difficulty.

Like Abraham, Jesus struggled mightily with God's call. In the garden of Gethsemane, he asked the Father if there was any other way, but in the end, he obediently walked up Mount Calvary to the cross. We can't know all the reasons that our Father is allowing bad things to happen to us, but like Jesus did, we can trust him in those difficult times. As we look at him and re-joice in what he did for us, we will have the joy and hope necessary—and the freedom from counterfeit gods—to follow the call of God when times seem at their darkest and most difficult.

TWO

Love Is Not All You Need

The Search for Love

The human longing for true love has always been celebrated in song and story, but in our contemporary culture it has been magnified to an astonishing degree. Musical theater is filled with many sunny love songs, but some reveal the dark side of this modern quest. In "Being Alive" from the musical *Company*, a man falls in love with a woman and sings that she will "need me too much . . . know me too well . . . pull me up short, and put me through hell." He insists, nonetheless, that only romance will "give me support for being alive, make me alive." He must go from one draining relationship to the next, because it is the only way he can feel alive. In the song "Bewitched" a woman admits that the man she's fallen for is a fool, and will let her down, but, she says, "I'm wild again, beguiled again, a simpering, whimpering child again." The singers are overdependent on being in love. Without a romantic relationship of some kind, even the wrong kind, their lives feel meaningless.

In the early days of my pastoral ministry, I met a woman named Sally, who'd had the misfortune of being born beautiful. Even in childhood she saw the power that she could wield with her physical attractiveness. At first she used her beauty to manipulate others, but eventually others used it to manipulate her. She came to feel that she was powerless and invisible unless some man was in love with her. She could not bear to be alone. As a result, she was willing to remain in relationships with men who were abusive.

Why did she endure such treatment? She had come to look to men for the kind of deep affirmation and acceptance that only God can provide. As a result, she became a slave to love. Nowadays we may hear someone say, "Oh, my boss is a slave master," but that is only a loose metaphor. Some bosses can make things hard on you, but real slave masters know no boundaries. They can literally do anything they want to you—beat you, rape you, or even kill you. In the same way, we know a good thing has become a counterfeit god when its demands on you exceed proper boundaries. Making an idol out of work may mean that you work until you ruin your health, or you break the laws in order to get ahead. Making an idol out of love may mean allowing the lover to exploit and abuse you, or it may cause terrible blindness to the pathologies in the relationship. An idolatrous attachment can lead you to break any promise, rationalize any indiscretion, or betray any other allegiance, in order to hold on to it. It may drive you to violate all good and proper boundaries. To practice idolatry is to be a slave.

There is a story in the Bible that illustrates how the quest for love can become a form of slavery. It is the story of Jacob and Leah in Genesis 29, and while very ancient, it has never been more relevant. It has always been possible to make romantic love and marriage into a counterfeit god, but we live in a culture that makes it even easier to mistake love for God, to be swept up by it, and to rest all our hopes for happiness upon it.

The Promise of the Messiah

As we saw in the last chapter, God came to Abraham and promised to redeem the world through his family, through a line of his descendents. Therefore, in every generation one child would be chosen to bear the line, to walk with God as head of the family, and to pass the faith on to the next generation. Then there would be another child that would carry on, and another, until the day when one of Abraham's descendents would be *the* Messiah himself.

Abraham fathered Isaac. Years later Isaac's wife, Rebekah, became pregnant with twins, and God spoke through a prophecy saying, "The elder will serve the younger" (Genesis 25:23). That meant that the second twin born had been chosen to carry on the Messianic line. In spite of the prophecy, Isaac set his heart on the older son, Esau, and favored him over the younger Jacob. Ironically, this was the same tragic mistake that God had saved Abraham from making, when he had called him to offer up his only son. Because of Isaac's favoritism, Esau grew up proud, spoiled, willful, and impulsive, while Jacob grew up cynical and bitter.

The time came for the aged Isaac to give the blessing to the head of the clan, which, in defiance of God's prophecy, he intended to give to Esau. But Jacob dressed up as his older brother, went in to his nearly blind father, and received the blessing from the unsuspecting Isaac. When Esau found out about it, he vowed to kill Jacob, and Jacob had to flee for his life into the wilderness.

Jacob's life was in ruins. He had lost his family and his inheritance. He would never see his mother and his father alive again. Jacob headed to the other side of the Fertile Crescent, where many of the relatives of his mother and his grandfather still lived. There he hoped at least to survive.

Jacob's Longing

Jacob escaped to his mother's family, and they took him in. His uncle Laban hired him as a shepherd of some of his flocks. Once Laban realized that Jacob had real ability as a manager, he offered him a management job. "What can I pay you to be in charge of my flocks?" he asked. Jacob's answer was one word: Rachel.

> Now Laban had two daughters; the name of the older was Leah, and the name of the younger was Rachel. Leah had weak eyes, but Rachel was lovely in form, and beautiful. Jacob was in love with Rachel and said, "I'll work for you seven years in return for your younger daughter Rachel." Laban said, "It's better that I give her to you than to some other man. Stay here with me." So Jacob served seven years to get Rachel, but they seemed like only a few days to him because of his love for her.
>
> Genesis 29:16–20

The Hebrew text says, literally, that Rachel had a great figure, and on top of that was beautiful. Jacob was more than smitten with her. Robert Alter, the great Hebrew literature scholar at Berkeley, points out the many signals in the text showing how lovesick and overwhelmed Jacob was with Rachel.[25] Jacob offered seven years' wages for her, which was, in the currency of the time, an enormous price for a bride. "But they seemed like only a few days to him because of his love for her (Verse 20)." "Then Jacob said to Laban, 'Give me my wife. My time is completed, and I want to lie with her. (Verse 21)'" Alter says that the Hebrew phrase is unusually bald, graphic, and sexual for ordinarily reticent ancient discourse. Imagine saying to a father even today, "I can't wait to have sex with your daughter. Give her to me now!" The narrator is showing us a man overwhelmed with emotional and sexual longing for one woman.

Why? Jacob's life was empty. He never had his father's love, he had lost his beloved mother's love, and he certainly had no sense of God's love and care. Then he beheld the most beautiful woman he had ever seen, and he must have said to himself, "If I had her, finally, something would be right in my miserable life. If I had her, it would fix things." All the longings of his heart for meaning and affirmation were fixed on Rachel.

Jacob was unusual for his time. Cultural historians tell us that in ancient times people didn't generally marry for love, they married for status. Nevertheless Jacob would not be rare today. Ernest Becker, who won the Pulitzer Prize for his book *The Denial of Death,* explained the various ways secular people have dealt with the loss of belief in God. Now that we think we are here by accident and not made for any purpose, how do we instill a sense of significance in our lives? One of the main ways is what Becker called "apocalyptic romance." We look to sex and romance to give us the transcendence and sense of meaning we used to get from faith in God. Talking about the modern secular person, he wrote:

> He still needed to feel heroic, to know that his life mattered in the scheme of things. . . . He still had to merge himself with some higher, self-absorbing meaning, in trust and gratitude. . . . If he no longer had God, how was he to do this? One of the first ways that occurred to him, as [Otto] Rank saw, was the "romantic solution." . . . The self-glorification that he needed in his innermost nature he now looked for in the love partner. The love partner becomes the divine ideal within which to fulfill one's life. All spiritual and moral needs now become focused in one individual. . . . In one word, the love object is God. . . . Man reached for a "thou" when the world-view of the great religious community overseen by God died. . . . [26] After all, what is it that we want when we elevate the love partner to the position of God? We want redemption—nothing less.[27]

That is exactly what Jacob did, and, as Becker points out, that is what millions of others are doing in our culture. The popular music and art of our society calls us to keep on doing it, to load all of the deepest needs of our hearts for significance and transcendence into romance and love. "You're nobody till somebody loves you," went the popular song, and we are an entire culture that has taken it literally. We maintain the fantasy that if we find our one true soul mate, everything wrong with us will be healed. But when our expectations and hopes reach that magnitude, as Becker says, "the love object is God." No lover, no human being, is qualified for that role. No one can live up to that. The inevitable result is bitter disillusionment.

The Power of Love

Some say that Becker's cultural analysis is dated. We now live in "the hookup culture," in which young people have turned sex into something ordinary, casual, and free from commitment. Fewer men and women actually date or have boyfriends and girlfriends. In the interest of gender equality, women have begun to say, "We deserve to have as much fun with our sexuality as guys do." There is growing peer pressure to engage in sex and not get too emotionally involved.[28] Surely, then, our culture is moving away from any hope in "apoca-

lyptic romance." Once we get over our lingering Puri-
tanism, the argument goes, sex will be no big deal.

Don't bet on it.

Laura Sessions Stepp, in her book *Unhooked*, found
that hookups left most young women unsatisfied,
though they are unwilling to admit this to their peers.
And the enormous stress our culture puts on physical
and sexual beauty belies any notion that sex is no big
deal. In the 1940s, C. S. Lewis heard from many of
his peers in the British academy that sex was nothing
but an appetite, like that for food. Once we recognized
this, they said, and began to simply have sex whenever
we wanted it, people would cease to be "driven mad"
by desire for love and sex. Lewis doubted this, and proposed a thought experiment.

> Suppose you come to a country where you could
> fill a theatre by simply bringing a covered plate
> on to the stage and then slowly lifting the cover
> so as to let every one see, just before the lights
> went out, that it contained a mutton chop or a
> bit of bacon, would you not think in that country
> something had gone wrong with the appetite for
> food? . . . One critic said that if he found a coun-
> try in which such strip-tease acts with food were
> popular, he would conclude that the people of
> that country were starving.[29]

However, Lewis goes on to argue, we are not starving for sex; there is more sex available than ever before. Yet pornography, the equivalent of striptease acts, is now a trillion-dollar industry. Sex and romantic love are therefore not "just an appetite" like food. They are far more meaningful to us than that. Evolutionary biologists explain that this is hardwired into our brains. Christians explain that our capacity for romantic love stems from our being in the image of God (Genesis 1:27–29; Ephesians 5:25–31). Perhaps it can be said that both are true.

In any case, romantic love is an object of enormous power for the human heart and imagination, and therefore can excessively dominate our lives. Even people who completely avoid romantic love out of bitterness or fear are actually being controlled by its power. I once knew a man who said he had been so disappointed by women that he now engaged only in no-commitment sexual encounters. No longer would he be manipulated by love, he boasted. In response, I argued that if you are so afraid of love that you *cannot* have it, you are just as enslaved as if you *must* have it. The person who can't have it will avoid people who would be wonderful partners. The person who must have it will choose partners who are ill-fitting to them or abusive. If you are too afraid of love *or* too enamored by it, it has assumed godlike power, distorting your perceptions and your life.

The Sting

Jacob's inner emptiness had made him vulnerable to the idolatry of romantic love. When he offered to work seven years for Rachel, nearly four times more than the ordinary price for a bride, the unscrupulous Laban saw how lovesick he was. He decided to take advantage of his condition. When Jacob asked if he could marry Rachel, Laban's response was deliberately vague. He never actually said, "Yes, it's a deal," but rather "It's better that you get her than some other man" (Genesis 29:19). Jacob wanted to hear the answer yes, and so he heard a yes. But it was not a yes. Laban merely said, "I think it is a good idea for you to marry Rachel."

Seven years passed, and Jacob came to Laban and said, "Now give me my wife." As was customary, there was a great wedding feast. In the middle of the celebration Laban brought Jacob's wife to him, heavily veiled. Already inebriated from the festivities, Jacob lay down with her and had sex with her. But "when morning came, there was Leah!" (Genesis 29:25) In the full light of day, Jacob looked and saw that the woman with whom he had consummated his marriage was Leah, the unattractive older sister of Rachel. Trembling with anger, Jacob went to Laban and said, "What is this you have done to me?" Laban replied calmly that he should have known that it was customary in their land for the older girl to be married before the younger girl. If Jacob was committed to work for an additional seven years, he added, he'd be happy to throw Rachel in as part of the deal. Stung and trapped, Jacob submitted to seven more years in order to marry Rachel as well as Leah.[30]

The Devastation of Idolatry

We may wonder how Jacob could have been so gullible, but Jacob's behavior was that of an addict. There are many ways that romantic love can function as a kind of drug to help us escape the reality of our lives. Sally, the beautiful woman who was trapped in abusive relationships, once said to me that "men were my alcohol. Only if I was on a man's arm could I face life and feel good about myself." Another example is the older man who abandons his spouse for a far younger woman, in a desperate effort to hide the reality that he is aging. Then there is the young man who finds a woman desirable only until she sleeps with him a couple of times, after which he loses interest in her. For him, women are simply a necessary commodity to help him feel desirable and powerful. Our fears and inner barrenness make love a narcotic, a way to medicate ourselves, and addicts always make foolish, destructive choices.

That is what had happened to Jacob. Rachel was not

just his wife, but his "savior." He wanted and needed Rachel so profoundly that he heard and saw only the things he wanted to hear and see. That is why he became vulnerable to Laban's deception. Later, Jacob's idolatry of Rachel created decades of misery in his family. He adored and favored Rachel's sons over Leah's, spoiling and embittering the hearts of all his children, and poisoning the family system. We have a phrase to describe someone who has fallen in love: "He worships the ground she walks on." How destructive this can be when it is literally the case.

We see how idolatry ravaged Jacob's life, but perhaps the greatest casualty of all is Leah. Leah is the older daughter, and the narrator gives us but one important detail about her. The text says that she had "weak or poor eyes." Some have assumed it meant she had bad eyesight. But the passage does not say, "Leah had weak eyes, but Rachel could see very well." It says Leah had weak eyes, but Rachel was beautiful. So "weakness" probably meant she was cross-eyed or literally unsightly in some way. The point is clear. Leah was particularly unattractive, and she had to live all of her life in the shadow of her sister, who was absolutely stunning.

As a result, her father, Laban, knew that no man was ever going to marry her or offer any money for her. For years he had wondered how he was going to get rid of her so that Rachel, who would bring a fine price, could be wed. In Jacob, Laban found the solution to his financial problem. He saw his opportunity, and he capitalized on it. But see what this meant for Leah—the daughter whom her father did not want was now a wife whom her husband did not want. "Jacob loved Rachel more than Leah" (Genesis 29:30). She was the girl that nobody wanted. [31]

Leah, then, had a hollow in her heart every bit as big as the hollow in Jacob's heart. And now she began to respond to it the same way Jacob had. She did to Jacob what Jacob had done to Rachel and what Isaac had done to Esau. She set her heart's hope on getting Jacob's love. The last verses here are some of the most plaintive you will find in the Bible.

When the LORD saw that Leah was not loved, he opened her womb, but Rachel was barren. Leah became pregnant and gave birth to a son. She named him Reuben, for she said, "It is because the LORD has seen my misery. Surely my husband will love me now." She conceived again, and when she gave birth to a son she said, "Because the LORD heard that I am not loved, he gave me this one too." So she named him Simeon. Again she conceived, and when she gave birth to a son she said, "Now at last my husband will become attached to me, because I

have borne him three sons." So he was named Levi.
She conceived again, and when she gave birth to a
son she said, "This time I will praise the LORD."
So she named him Judah. Then she stopped having
children.

Genesis 29:31–35[32]

What was she doing? She was trying to find happiness and an identity through traditional family values. Having sons, especially in those days, was the best way to do that; but it was not working. She had set all of her hopes and dreams on her husband. "If I have babies and sons, then my husband will come to love me, and then finally my unhappy life will be fixed," she thought. But instead, every birth pushed her down deeper into a hell of loneliness. Every single day she was condemned to see the man she most longed for in the arms of the one in whose shadow she had lived all of her life. Every day was like another knife in the heart.

Cosmic Disillusionment

At this point in the story, many contemporary readers will be wondering: "Where are all the spiritual heroes in this story? Whom am I supposed to be emulating? What is the moral of the story?"

The reason for our confusion is that we usually read

the Bible as a series of disconnected stories, each with a "moral" for how we should live our lives. It is not. Rather, it comprises a single story, telling us how the human race got into its present condition, and how God through Jesus Christ has come and will come to put things right. In other words, the Bible doesn't give us a god at the top of a moral ladder saying, "If you try hard to summon up your strength and live right, you can make it up!" Instead, the Bible repeatedly shows us weak people who don't deserve God's grace, don't seek it, and don't appreciate it even after they have received it. If that is the great biblical story arc into which every individual scriptural narrative fits, then what do we learn from this story?

We learn that through all of life there runs a ground note of cosmic disappointment. You are never going to lead a wise life until you understand that. Jacob said, "If I can just get Rachel, everything will be okay." And he goes to bed with the one who he thinks is Rachel, and literally, the Hebrew says, "in the morning, behold, it was Leah" (Genesis 29:25). One commentator noted about this verse, "This is a miniature of our disillusionment, experienced from Eden onwards."[33] What does that mean? With all due respect to this woman (from whom we have much to learn), it means that no matter what we put our hopes in, in the morning, *it is always Leah, never Rachel.*

Nobody has ever said this better than C. S. Lewis in *Mere Christianity*:

> Most people, if they have really learned to look into their own hearts, would know that they do want, and want acutely, something that cannot be had in this world. There are all sorts of things in this world that offer to give it to you, but they never quite keep their promise. The longings which arise in us when we first fall in love, or first think of some foreign country, or first take up some subject that excites us, are longings which no marriage, no travel, no learning, can really satisfy. I am not now speaking of what would be ordinarily called unsuccessful marriages, or holidays, or learned careers. I am speaking of the best possible ones. There was something we have grasped at, in that first moment of longing, which just fades away in the reality. I think everyone knows what I mean. The wife may be a good wife, and the hotels and scenery may have been excellent, and chemistry may be a very interesting job: but something has evaded us.[34]

If you get married as Jacob did, putting the weight of all your deepest hopes and longings on the person you are marrying, you are going to crush him or her with your expectations. It will distort your life and your spouse's life in a hundred ways. No person, not even the best one, can give your soul all it needs. You are going to think you have gone to bed with Rachel, and you will get up and it will always be Leah. This cosmic disappointment and disillusionment is there in all of life, but we especially feel it in the things upon which we most set our hopes.

When you finally realize this, there are four things you can do. You can blame the things that are disappointing you and try to move on to better ones. That's the way of continued idolatry and spiritual addiction. The second thing you can do is blame yourself and beat yourself and say, "I have somehow been a failure. I see everybody else is happy. I don't know why I am not happy. There is something wrong with me." That's the way of self-loathing and shame. Third, you can blame the world. You can say, "Curses on the entire opposite sex," in which case you make yourself hard, cynical, and empty. Lastly, you can, as C. S. Lewis says at the end of his great chapter on hope, reorient the entire focus of your life toward God. He concludes, "If I find in myself a desire which no experience in this world can satisfy, the most probable explanation is that I was made for another world [something supernatural and eternal]."[35]

Male and Female Idolatries

Jacob is after "apocalyptic sex." Leah, the tradition-
alist, is having babies and trying to find her identity
in being a wife. But they are both frustrated. Ernest
Becker explains why:

> The failure of romantic love as a solution to
> human problems is so much a part of modern
> man's frustration. . . . No human relationship
> can bear the burden of godhood. . . . However
> much we may idealize and idolize him [the love
> partner], he inevitably reflects earthly decay and
> imperfection. . . . After all, what is it that we
> want when we elevate the love partner to this po-
> sition? We want to be rid of our faults, of our
> feeling of nothingness. We want to be justified,
> to know our existence has not been in vain. We
> want redemption—nothing less. Needless to say,
> human partners cannot give this.[36]

Both the stereotypically male and female idolatries
regarding romantic love are dead ends. It is often said
that "men use love to get sex, women use sex to get
love." As in all stereotypes there is some truth to this,
but this story shows that both of these counterfeit gods
disappoint. Because Jacob sought to get his life vali-

dated from having a physically beautiful wife, he gave his heart to a woman toward whose immaturity and shortcomings he was blind. Leah's counterfeit god was not sex. She obviously had access to her husband's body, but not to his love and commitment. She wanted him to be "attached" to her, to have his soul cleave to her. But he did not. Her life became bound in shallows and miseries.

In our modern culture, there has been a growing awareness that many women are victims of "commitment idolatry." In a *New York Times* review of the movie *He's Just Not That Into You,* Manohla Dargis laments that Hollywood keeps giving us movies about young women "where female desire now largely seems reserved for shoes, wedding bells, and babies." One of the characters goes out on her first date and afterward calls a friend to tell her she thought the evening went well. Meanwhile, the man is home calling up another woman.[37]

The writer is right to point out that women who have made an idol of romance and a big wedding to Prince Charming become enslaved to their own desires. She advises women to abandon their typical love-idolatries and take up the male version. But, as we have seen, *all* idolatries enslave. Male love idolatries make them addicted to being independent, so they can "play the field." Female love idolatries, as the reviewer points out, make them addicted and dependent—vulnerable and easily manipulated. Both are a form of slavery, both blind us so we can't make wise life choices, both distort our lives. So what can we do?

Leah's Breakthrough

Leah is the one person in this sad story to make some spiritual progress, though this happens only at its very end. Look first at what God does in her. One of the things Hebrew scholars notice is that in all of Leah's statements, she was calling on *the LORD*. She used the name *Yahweh*. "*The Lord* [Yahweh] has seen my misery," she says in verse 32. How did she know about Yahweh?

Elohim was the generic Hebrew word for God. All cultures at that time had some general idea of God or gods, but Yahweh was the name of the God who had revealed himself to Abraham, and later to Moses. He was the one who told Abraham that he would bless the earth through his line. The only way Leah could have known about *Yahweh* was if Jacob had told her about the promise to his grandfather. So even though she was struggling and confused, she was nonetheless reaching out to a personal God of grace.

After years of childbearing, however, there's a breakthrough. When Leah gave birth to her last son, Judah, she said, "*This* time, I will praise the LORD." There was a defiance in that claim. It was a different declaration from the ones she had made after the other births. There was no mention of husband or child. It appears that finally, she had taken her heart's deepest hopes off of her husband and her children, and had put them on the Lord. Jacob and Laban had stolen Leah's life, but when she gave her heart finally to the Lord, she got her life back.

The True Bridegroom

We shouldn't just look at what God did in her. We have to also look at what God did *for* her. Leah might have had a sense that there was something special about this last child. She may have had an intuition that God had done something for her. And he had. Certainly, the writer of Genesis knew it. This child was Judah, and in Genesis 49 we are told that it is through him that the true King, the Messiah, will someday come. God had come to the girl that nobody wanted, the unloved, and made *her* the ancestral mother of Jesus. Salvation came into the world, not through beautiful Rachel, but through the unwanted one, the unloved one.

Does God just like to root for underdogs? No, this wonderful gift to Leah meant far more than that. The text says that when the Lord saw that Leah was not loved, *he* loved her. God was saying, "I am the real bridegroom. I am the husband of the husbandless. I am the father of the fatherless." This is the God who saves by grace. The gods of moralistic religions favor the successful and the overachievers. They are the ones who climb the moral ladder up to heaven. But the God of the Bible is the one who comes down into this world to accomplish a salvation and give us a grace we could never attain ourselves. He loves the unwanted, the weak and unloved. He is not just a king and we are the subjects; he is not just a shepherd and we are the sheep. He is a husband and we are his spouse. He is ravished with us—even those of us whom no one else notices.

And here is the power to overcome our idolatries. There are many people in the world who have not found a romantic partner, and they need to hear the Lord say, "I am the true Bridegroom. There is only one set of arms that will give you all your heart's desire, and await you at the end of time, if only you turn to me. And know that I love you now." However, it is not just those without spouses who need to see that God is our ultimate spouse, but those *with* spouses as well. They need this in order to save their marriage from the crushing weight of their divine expectations. If you marry someone expecting them to be like a god, it is only inevitable that they will disappoint you. It's not that you should try to love your spouse less, but rather that you should know and love God more. How can we know God's love so deeply that we release our lovers and spouses from our stifling expectations? By looking at the one to whom Leah's life points.

The Man Nobody Wanted

When God came to earth in Jesus Christ, he was truly the son of Leah. He became the man nobody wanted. He was born in a manger. He had no beauty that we should desire him (Isaiah 53:2). He came to his own and his own received him not (John 1:11). And at the end, everybody abandoned him. Jesus cried out even to his Father: "Why have you forsaken me?"

Why did he become Leah's son? Why did he become the man nobody wanted? For you and for me. He took upon himself our sins and died in our place. If we are deeply moved by the sight of his love for us, it detaches our hearts from other would-be saviors. We stop trying to redeem ourselves through our pursuits and relationships, because we are already redeemed. We stop trying to make others into saviors, because we have a Savior.

The only way to dispossess the heart of an old affection is by the expulsive power of a new one. . . .
Thus . . . it is not enough . . . to hold out to the

world the mirror of its own imperfections. It is not enough to come forth with a demonstration of the evanescent character of your enjoyments . . . to speak to the conscience . . . of its follies. . . . Rather, try every legitimate method of finding access to your hearts for the love of Him who is greater than the world.[38]

One day Sally told me how she got her life back. She went to a counselor who rightly pointed out that she had been looking to men for her identity, for her "salvation." Instead, the counselor proposed, she should get a career and become financially independent as a way of building up her self-esteem. The woman agreed wholeheartedly that she needed to stand on her own two feet economically, but she resisted the advice about finding self-esteem. "I was being advised to give up a common female idolatry and take on a common male idolatry," she said. "But I didn't want to have my self-worth dependent on career success any more than on men. I wanted to be free."

How did she do it? She came across Colossians 3, where Saint Paul writes: "Your life is hidden with Christ in God . . . and when Christ who is your life appears, you will appear with him in glory" (Colossians 3:1–4). She came to realize that neither men nor career nor anything else should be "her life" or identity. What mattered was not what men thought of her, or career success, but what Christ had done for her and how he loved her. So when she saw a man was interested in her, she would silently say in her heart toward him, "You may turn out to be a great guy, and maybe even my husband, but you cannot ever be *my life*. Only Christ is my life." When she began to do this, like Leah, she got her life back. This spiritual discipline gave her the ability to set boundaries and make good choices, and eventually to love a man for himself, and not simply to use men to bolster her self-image.

She had answered the question that we all must address in order to live our lives the way we should: Who can I turn to who is so beautiful that he will enable me to escape all counterfeit gods? There is only one answer to this question. As the poet George Herbert wrote, looking at Jesus on the Cross: "Thou art my loveliness, my life, my light, Beauty alone to me."[39]

THREE

✦✧✦✧✦

MONEY CHANGES EVERYTHING

Naked Greed

In 2005, investment bank Credit Suisse aggressively promoted loans to resorts. These loans offered instant personal proceeds to borrowers and high yields to institutional investors. In response, the founder and largest shareholder of the Yellowstone Club, a private ski resort catering to the very wealthy in the mountains of Montana, took out a $375 million loan. Two hundred nine million immediately went to his personal accounts, as the loan agreement permitted. Credit Suisse did little to appraise the ability of the borrower to repay, since it had no money of its own at risk. The loan was packaged and sold as part of a "collateralized loan obligation," transferring all potential problems to institutional investors such as pension funds who were buying loan products whose risks were vastly underestimated by the sellers. Credit Suisse did about six resort deals like this from 2002 to 2006, totaling close to $3 billion.

By 2007, however, the Yellowstone Club was in serious financial trouble. Routinely poor management was aggravated by the heavy debt service on the Credit Suisse loan. When the recession hit and real estate values declined, the club filed for bankruptcy. Credit Suisse, who had "first lien" rights, proposed an interim funding plan to "mothball" the club, which would have thrown hundreds of employees out of work. The vendors, waitresses, gardeners, and lift operators of the small towns of Montana, who had few other employment options, were about to take a terrible economic hit.

Fortunately, a Montana bankruptcy judge saw through what had happened. He blasted Credit Suisse and the club owner for "naked greed" and a "predatory loan" that had made them rich while laying all the risk and consequences on the backs of the working class people of the area. He stripped Credit Suisse of its first lien position, a rare act in bankruptcy court. The judge's rulings made it possible for another buyer to purchase the club, and so many jobs were saved.[40]

A journalist reporting this story called this a snapshot of the "economic zeitgeist" of the age. The new explosion in executive salaries, the increased emphasis on luxury goods, the rapacious deals that make millions for the deal makers at the expense of thousands of common workers, the lack of concern about steep debt—all of these things represent profound social changes in our society. Paul Krugman writes about these changes in attitudes:

> We should not think of it as a market trend like the rising value of waterfront property, but as something more like the sexual revolution of the 1960s—a relaxation of old strictures, a new permissiveness, but in this case the permissiveness is financial rather than sexual. Sure enough, John Kenneth Galbraith described the honest executive of 1967 as being one who "eschews the lovely, available, and even naked woman by whom he is intimately surrounded. . . . Management does not go out ruthlessly to reward itself. . . ." By the end of the 1990s, the executive motto might as well have been, "If it feels good, do it."[41]

We Can't See Our Own Greed

Ernest Becker wrote that our culture would replace God with sex and romance. Even earlier, Friedrich Nietzsche had a different theory. He wrote that, with the absence of God growing in Western culture, we would replace God with money.

> What induces one man to use false weights, another to set his house on fire after having insured it for more than its value, while three-fourths of our upper classes indulge in legalized fraud . . . what gives rise to all this? It is not real want—for their existence is by no means precarious . . . but they are urged on day and night by a terrible impatience at seeing their wealth pile up so slowly, and by an equally terrible longing and love for these heaps of gold. . . . What once was done "for the love of God" is now done for the love of money, i.e., for the love of that which at present affords us the highest feeling of power and a good conscience.[42]

In short, Nietzsche foretold that money in Western culture would become perhaps its main counterfeit god.

Innumerable writers and thinkers have been pointing out "the culture of greed" that has been eating away at our souls and has brought about economic collapse. Yet no one thinks that change is around the corner. Why? It's because greed and avarice are especially hard to see in ourselves.

Some years ago I was doing a seven-part series of talks on the Seven Deadly Sins at a men's breakfast. My wife, Kathy, told me, "I'll bet that the week you deal with greed you will have your lowest attendance." She was right. People packed it out for "Lust" and "Wrath" and even for "Pride." But nobody thinks they are greedy. As a pastor I've had people come to me to confess that they struggle with almost every kind of sin. Almost. I cannot recall anyone ever coming to me and saying, "I spend too much money on myself. I think my greedy lust for money is harming my family, my soul, and people around me." Greed hides itself from the victim. The money god's modus operandi includes blindness to your own heart.

Why can't anyone in the grip of greed see it? The counterfeit god of money uses powerful sociological and psychological dynamics. Everyone tends to live in a particular socioeconomic bracket. Once you are able to afford to live in a particular neighborhood, send your children to its schools, and participate in its social life, you will find yourself surrounded by quite a number of people who have more money than you. You don't compare yourself to the rest of the world, you compare yourself to those in your bracket. The human heart always wants to justify itself and this is one of the easiest ways. You say, "I don't live as well as him or her or them. My means are modest compared to theirs."

You can reason and think like that no matter how lavishly you are living. As a result, most Americans think of themselves as middle class, and only 2 percent call themselves "upper class."[43] But the rest of the world is not fooled. When people visit here from other parts of the globe, they are staggered to see the level of materialistic comfort that the majority of Americans have come to view as a necessity.

Jesus warns people far more often about greed than about sex, yet almost no one thinks they are guilty of it. Therefore we should all begin with a working hypothesis that "this could easily be a problem for me." If greed hides itself so deeply, no one should be confident that it is not a problem for them. How can we recognize and become free from the power of money to blind us?

The Seductive Power of Money

Jesus entered Jericho and was passing through. A man was there by the name of Zacchaeus; he was a chief tax collector and was wealthy.

Luke 19:1–2

With brief but telling strokes, the gospel of Luke introduces us to Zacchaeus. He was a "tax collector" who was shunned by his community. Even today, people who work for the IRS don't advertise it at parties, but we must understand what this meant at that time and place. Israel was a conquered nation, under military occupation. Their conquerors, the Romans, levied oppressive taxes on each colony as a means for transferring most of the nation's wealth and capital to Rome and its citizens. This left the colonial societies impoverished, which kept them subjugated. The only people who lived in comfort and ease in Israel were the Romans who ruled and their local collaborators, the tax collectors. The tax system depended on officials who were charged with extracting, for their Roman overlords, the tax income from each region targeted for collection. Everyone despised them. The people called Zacchaeus a "sinner" (Verse 7), which meant apostate or outcast. If you want to get a sense of how these functionaries were regarded, think of what people thought of the collaborators who, under the Nazis, oppressed their own people during World War II; think of drug lords who get rich enslaving thousands of the weakest people of the inner city; think of modern-day "robber barons" who buy out and then destroy companies, or sell common people mortgages they cannot afford, while making millions for themselves. Now you can understand the stature of tax collectors at this time.

Why would anyone take such a job as a tax collector? What could seduce a man to betray his family and country and live as a pariah in his own society? The answer was—money. The incentive the Romans offered tax collectors was almost irresistible. Backed by military force, the tax collector was allowed to demand much more money from his fellow Jews than he had contracted to pay the government. Today, we call this extortion. It was extremely lucrative. Tax collectors were the wealthiest people in society, and the most hated.

One of the reasons Luke brought Zacchaeus to our attention was that he was not just a regular tax collector. He was an *architelones* (Verse 2), literally, the *arch*–tax collector. It was not surprising that we find him in Jericho, a major customs center. As a head of the entire system he would have been one of its wealthiest and the most hated members. He lived in a time, unlike ours, when there was a stigma attached to conspicuous consumption and to reveling in wealth. But that didn't matter to him. He had sacrificed everything else in order to get money.

Money as a Master

Paul says greed is a form of idolatry (Colossians 3:5; Ephesians 5:5). Luke is teaching us the same thing in his gospel.[44] In Luke 12:15 Jesus says to listeners: "Watch out! Be on your guard against all kinds of greed, for a man's life does not consist in the abundance of his possessions." What is greed? In the surrounding passages of Luke 11 and 12, Jesus warned people about worrying over their possessions. For Jesus, greed is not only love of money, but excessive anxiety about it. He lays out the reason our emotions are so powerfully controlled by our bank account—"a man's life does not consist in the abundance of his possessions." To "consist" of your possessions is to be defined by what you own and consume. The term describes a personal identity based on money. It refers to people who, if they lose their wealth, do not have a "self" left, for their personal worth is based on their financial worth. Later Jesus comes right out and calls this what it is.

> *"No servant can serve two masters; either he will hate the one and love the other, or he will be devoted to the one and despise the other. You cannot serve both God and money." The Pharisees, who loved money, heard all this and were sneering at Jesus. He said to them, "You are the ones who justify yourselves in the eyes of men, but God knows your hearts. What is highly valued among men is detestable in God's sight."*
>
> Luke 16:13–15

Jesus uses all the basic biblical metaphors for idolatry and applies them to greed and money. According to the Bible, idolaters do three things with their idols.

They love them, trust them, and obey them.[45] "Lovers of money" are those who find themselves daydreaming and fantasizing about new ways to make money, new possessions to buy, and looking with jealousy on those who have more than they do. "Trusters of money" feel they have control of their lives and are safe and secure because of their wealth.

Idolatry also makes us "servants of money." Just as we serve earthly kings and magistrates, so we "sell our souls" to our idols. Because we look to them for our significance (love) and security (trust) we *have* to have them, and therefore we are driven to serve and, essentially, obey them. When Jesus says that we "serve" money, he uses a word that means the solemn, covenantal service rendered to a king. If you live for money you are a slave. If, however, God becomes the center of your life, that dethrones and demotes money. If your identity and security is in God, it can't control you through worry and desire. It is one or the other. You either serve God, or you become open to slavery to Mammon.

Nowhere is this slavery more evident than in the blindness of greedy people to their own materialism. Notice that in Luke 12 Jesus says, "Watch out! Be on your guard against all kinds of greed." That is a remarkable statement. Think of another traditional sin that the Bible warns against—adultery. Jesus doesn't say, "Be careful you aren't committing adultery!" He doesn't have to. When you are in bed with someone else's spouse—you know it. Halfway through you don't say, "Oh, wait a minute! I think this is adultery!" You know it is. Yet, even though it is clear that the world is filled with greed and materialism, almost no one thinks it is true of them. They are in denial.

Can we look at Zacchaeus any longer and ask, "How could he have betrayed and harmed so many people? How could he have been willing to be so hated? How could he have been so blinded by money to do all that and live like that?" Zacchaeus is just one example of what Jesus has been teaching all through the book of Luke. Money is one of the most common counterfeit gods there is. When it takes hold of your heart it blinds you to what is happening, it controls you through your anxieties and lusts, and it brings you to put it ahead of all other things.

The Beginnings of Grace

[Zacchaeus] wanted to see who Jesus was, but being a short man he could not, because of the crowd. So he ran ahead and climbed a sycamore-fig tree to see him, since Jesus was coming that way. When Jesus reached the spot, he looked up and said to him, "Zacchaeus, come down immediately. I must stay

at your house today." So he came down at once and
welcomed him gladly. All the people saw this and
began to mutter, "He has gone to be the guest of a
'sinner.'"

Luke 19:3–7

Zacchaeus was a short man, but why couldn't
a short man stand on the road in front of the taller
people? Obviously, the people would not give way to
him. In response, Zacchaeus did a surprising thing.
He climbed a tree. We must appreciate the significance
of this. In traditional cultures it was not freedom and
rights that mattered but honor and dignity. For any
grown male to climb up into a tree would have invited
enormous ridicule. Surely a person like Zacchaeus, who
was already despised and a short man as well, would be
more careful to act in a way that was fitting to a digni-
fied personage. So why did he do it? Luke tells us, "He
wanted to see who Jesus was." Zacchaeus was eager to
connect to Jesus. *Eager* may be too weak a word. His
willingness to climb a tree signifies something close to
desperation.

Jesus came along and he saw a crowd of mainly
respectable, religious people, all of whom felt superior to prostitutes and tax collectors (Luke 19:7;
Matthew 21:31). Instead of addressing any of them,
he singled out the most notorious "sinner" in the

whole throng. Zacchaeus was the *arch*collector, the worst of all. Yet right in the face of this very moral crowd, he selected this man not only to talk to but to eat with. In that culture, eating with someone meant friendship. Everyone was offended, but Jesus did not care. He said, "Zacchaeus, I don't want to go to their houses, but to yours." And Zacchaeus welcomed him home with joy.

This simple interchange could not have been more instructive for us. Zacchaeus did not approach Jesus with pride but with humility. He did not stand on his dignity and wealth; instead he put aside his station in life and was willing to be ridiculed in order to get a glimpse of Jesus. Ultimately, it was not Zacchaeus who asked Jesus into his life, but Jesus who asked Zacchaeus into his. You can almost hear Jesus laugh as he says it. "Zacchaeus! Yes, you! It's *you* I'm going home with today!" Jesus knew how outrageous his action looked to the crowd, how it contradicted everything they knew about religion, and how startling it was to the little man himself who was up in the tree.

When Zacchaeus saw that Jesus had chosen the least virtuous person in the crowd—himself—for a personal relationship, his whole spiritual understanding began to change. Though it is unlikely that he had a clear, conscious understanding of this, he began to realize that God's salvation was by grace, not through moral achievement or performance. That realization went through him like lightning, and he welcomed Jesus with joy.

Grace and Money

But Zacchaeus stood up and said to the Lord, "Look, Lord! Here and now I give half of my possessions to the poor, and if I have cheated anybody out of anything, I will pay back four times the amount." Jesus said to him, "Today salvation has come to this house, because this man, too, is a son of Abraham. For the Son of Man came to seek and to save what was lost."

Luke 19:8–10

Zacchaeus wanted to follow Jesus, and immediately he realized that, if he was to do that, money was an issue. So he made two remarkable promises.

He promised to give away 50 percent of his income to the poor. This was far beyond the 10 percent giving that the Mosaic law required. Today, to give away even 10 percent of our income to charity seems an enormous sum, though wealthy people could do much more and still live comfortably. Zacchaeus knew that when he made this offer. His heart had been affected. Since he knew salvation was not through the law, but through grace, he did not aim to live by only fulfilling the letter of the law. He wanted to go beyond it.

There have been times when people have come to me as their pastor, and asked about "tithing," giving away a tenth of their annual income. They notice that in the Old Testament there are many clear commands that believers should give away 10 percent. But in the New Testament, specific, quantitative requirements for giving are less prominent. They often asked me, "You don't think that now, in the New Testament, believers are absolutely required to give away ten percent, do you?" I shake my head no, and they give a sigh of relief. But then I quickly add, "I'll tell you why you don't see the tithing requirement laid out clearly in the New Testament. Think. Have we received more of God's revelation, truth, and grace than the Old Testament believers, or less?" Usually there is uncomfortable silence. "Are we more 'debtors to grace' than they were, or less? Did Jesus 'tithe' his life and blood to save us or did he give it all?" Tithing is a minimum standard for Christian believers. We certainly wouldn't want to be in a position of giving away less of our income than those who had so much less of an understanding of what God did to save them.

Zacchaeus's second promise did not have to do so much with charity and mercy but with justice. He had made a great deal of money by cheating. There were many people from whom he had taken exorbitant revenues. Here again, the Mosaic law made a provision. Leviticus 5:16 and Numbers 5:7 directed that if you had stolen anything, you had to make restitution with interest. You had to give it back with 20 percent interest. However, Zacchaeus wanted to do far more. He would give back "four times the amount" he had stolen. That's 300 percent interest.

In response to these promises, Jesus said, "Salvation has come to this house." Notice, he didn't say, "If you live like this, salvation will come to this house." No, it *has* come. God's salvation does not come in response to a changed life. A changed life comes in response to the salvation, offered as a free gift.

That was the reason for Zacchaeus's new heart and life. If salvation had been something earned through obedience to the moral code, then Zacchaeus's question would have been "How much *must* I give?" However, these promises were responses to lavish, generous grace, so his question was "How much *can* I give?" He realized that while being financially rich, he had been spiritually bankrupt, but Jesus had poured out spiritual riches on him freely. He went from being an oppressor of the poor to being a champion of justice. He went from accruing wealth at the expense of the people around him to serving others at the expense of his wealth. Why? Jesus had replaced money as Zacchaeus's savior, and so money went back to being merely that, just money. It was now a tool for doing good, for serving people. Now that his identity and security were rooted in Christ, he had more money than he needed. The grace of God had transformed his attitude toward his wealth.

Grace and Deep Idols

To understand how Zacchaeus's heart began to change, we should consider that counterfeit gods come in clusters, making the idolatry structure of the heart complex. There are "deep idols" within the heart beneath the more concrete and visible "surface idols" that we serve.[46]

Sin in our hearts affects our basic motivational drives so they become idolatrous, "deep idols." Some people are strongly motivated by a desire for influence and power, while others are more excited by approval and appreciation. Some want emotional and physical comfort more than anything else, while still others want security, the control of their environment. People with the deep idol of power do not mind being unpopular in order to gain influence. People who are most motivated by approval are the opposite—they will gladly lose power and control as long as everyone thinks well of them. Each deep idol—power, approval, comfort, or control—generates a different set of fears and a different set of hopes.

"Surface idols" are things such as money, our spouse, or children, through which our deep idols seek fulfillment. We are often superficial in the analysis of our idol structures. For example, money can be a surface idol that serves to satisfy more foundational impulses. Some people want lots of money as a way to control their world and life. Such people usually don't spend much money and live very modestly. They keep it all safely saved and invested, so they can feel completely secure in the world. Others want money for access to social circles and to make themselves beautiful and attractive. These people *do* spend their money on themselves in lavish ways. Other people want money because it gives them so much power over others. In every case, money functions as an idol and yet, because of various deep idols, it results in very different patterns of behavior.

The person using money to serve a deep idol of control will often feel superior to people using money to attain power or social approval. In every case, however, money-idolatry enslaves and distorts lives. Another pastor at my church once counseled a married couple who had severe conflicts over how they handled money. The wife considered the husband a miser. One day the pastor was speaking one-on-one to the husband who was complaining bitterly about what a spendthrift his spouse was. "She is so selfish, spending so much on clothes and appearance!" He saw clearly how her need to look attractive to others influenced her use of money. The pastor then introduced him to the concept of surface and deep idols. "Do you see that by *not* spending or giving away anything, by socking away every penny, you are being just as selfish? You are 'spending' absolutely everything on your need to feel secure, protected, and in control." Fortunately for the counselor, the man was shocked rather than angered. "I'd never thought of it like that," he said, and things began to change in the marriage.

This is why idols cannot be dealt with by simply eliminating surface idols like money or sex. We can look at them and say, "I need to de-emphasize this in my life. I must not let this drive me. I will stop it." Direct appeals like that won't work, because the deep idols have to be dealt with at the heart level. There is only one way to change at the heart level and that is through faith in the gospel.

The Poverty of Christ

In 2 Corinthians 8 and 9 Paul asks a church to give an offering to the poor. Though he is an apostle with authority, he writes:, "I say this not by way of command" (2 Corinthians 8:8). He means: "I don't want to order you. I don't want this offering to be simply the response to a demand." He doesn't put pressure directly on the will and say, "I'm an apostle, so do what I say." Rather, he wants to see the "genuineness of your love," and then writes these famous words:

For you know the grace of our Lord Jesus Christ, that though he was rich, yet for your sake he became poor, so that you by his poverty might become rich.

2 Corinthians 8:9

Jesus, the God-Man, had infinite wealth, but if he had held on to it, we would have died in our spiritual poverty. That was the choice—if he stayed rich, we would die poor. If he died poor, we could become rich. Our sins would be forgiven, and we would be admitted into the family of God. Paul was not giving this church a mere ethical precept, exhorting them to stop loving money so much and become more generous. Rather, he recapitulated the gospel.

This is what Paul was saying. Jesus gave up all his treasure in heaven, in order to make you his treasure—for you are a treasured people (1 Peter 2:9–10). When you see him dying to make you his treasure, that will make him yours. Money will cease to be the currency of your significance and security, and you will want to bless others with what you have. To the degree that you grasp the gospel, money will have no dominion over you. Think on his costly grace until it changes you into a generous people.

The solution to stinginess is a reorientation to the generosity of Christ in the gospel, how he poured out his wealth for you. Now you don't have to worry about money—the Cross proves God's care for you and gives you the security. Now you don't have to envy anyone else's money. Jesus's love and salvation confers on you a remarkable status—one that money cannot give you. Money cannot save you from tragedy, or give you control in a chaotic world. Only God can do that. What breaks the power of money over us is not just redoubled effort to follow the example of Christ. Rather, it is deepening your understanding of the salvation of Christ, what you have in him, and then living out the changes that that understanding makes in your heart—the seat of your mind, will, and emotions. Faith in the gospel restructures our motivations, our self-understanding and identity, our view of the world. Behavioral compliance to rules without a complete change of heart will be superficial and fleeting.

Man Must Have an Idol

Andrew Carnegie became one of the wealthiest men in the world when his steel company, the forerunner

of U.S. Steel, became the most profitable business enterprise in the world. Early on in his success, at only
age thirty-three, Carnegie took a ruthless evalua-
tion of his own heart and produced a "note to self"
memorandum.

Man must have an idol—The amassing of wealth is
one of the worst species of idolatry. No idol more
debasing than the worship of money. Whatever
I engage in I must push inordinately therefore
should I be careful to choose the life which will
be the most elevating in character. To continue
much longer overwhelmed by business cares and
with most of my thoughts wholly upon the way
to make more money in the shortest time, must
degrade me beyond hope of permanent recovery.
I will resign business at Thirty five, but during
the ensuing two years, I wish to spend the af-
ternoons in securing instruction, and in reading
systematically.[47]

The candor and self-knowledge in this note is remarkable, and one of his biographers, Joseph Frazier,
commented, "Neither Rockefeller, nor Ford, nor Morgan could have written this note, nor would they have
understood the man who did."[48] Nevertheless, despite
his insight into his own heart, Carnegie obviously did

not "resign business" two years later, and many of the very character-degrading effects he feared worked themselves out in his life.

> Although Carnegie built 2,059 libraries . . . a steelworker, speaking for many, told an interviewer, "We didn't want him to build a library for us, we would rather have had higher wages." At that time steelworkers worked twelve-hour shifts on floors so hot they had to nail wooden platforms under their shoes. Every two weeks they toiled an inhuman twenty-four-hour shift, and then they got their sole day off. The best housing they could afford was crowded and filthy. Most died in their forties or earlier, from accidents or disease. . . . [49]

Bill, whom we met in the introduction, had lost a great deal of money during financial downturn of 2008–2009, after having become a Christian three years before. "If this had happened to me before I became a Christian, I would have hated myself, it would have driven me back to the bottle, and maybe to suicide," he said. At one time Bill could only feel like a person of worth and value if he was making money. He knew that if he had been in that kind of a spiritual relationship with money during the financial crisis, he would have lost all his sense of significance and meaning.[50] But his identity had shifted. It had ceased to rest in being successful and affluent and had come to be grounded in the grace and love of Jesus Christ. That was why he could say despite his losses, "Today, I can tell you honestly, I've never been happier in my life."

Andrew Carnegie knew that money was an idol in his heart, but he didn't know how to root it out. It can't be removed, only replaced. It must be supplanted by the one who, though rich, became poor, so that we might truly be rich.

FOUR

✦✧✦

THE SEDUCTION OF SUCCESS

Fast-Fading Satisfaction

Pop legend Madonna describes the seduction of success in her own words.

I have an iron will, and all of my will has always been to conquer some horrible feeling of inadequacy. . . . I push past one spell of it and discover myself as a special human being and then I get to another stage and think I'm mediocre and uninteresting. . . . Again and again. My drive in life is from this horrible fear of being mediocre. And that's always pushing me, pushing me. Because even though I've become Somebody, I still have to prove that I'm *Somebody*. My struggle has never ended and it probably never will.[51]

The Seduction of Success

For Madonna, success is like drug that gives her a sense of consequence and worth, but the high quickly wears off and she needs a repeat dose. She must prove herself again and again. The driving force behind this is not joy but fear.

In the movie *Chariots of Fire*, one of the main characters is an Olympic sprinter who eloquently articulates the same philosophy. When asked why he runs, he says he does not do it because he loves it. "I'm more of an addict . . . ," he replies. Later, before running the hundred-meter Olympic event, he sighs: "Contentment! I'm twenty-four and I've never known it. I'm forever in pursuit and I don't even know what it is I'm chasing. . . . I'll raise my eyes and look down that corridor, four feet wide, with ten lonely seconds to justify my whole existence . . . but will I?"[52] Not long before film director Sydney Pollack died, there was an article written about his inability to slow down and enjoy his final years with his loved ones. Though he was unwell, and the grueling process of filmmaking was wearing him down, "he couldn't justify his existence if he stopped." He explained, "Every time I finish a picture, I feel like I've done what I'm supposed to do in the sense that I've earned my stay for another year or so."[53] But then he had to start over.

"Achievement is the alcohol of our time," says Mary

Bell, a counselor who works with high-level executives. She goes on:

> These days, the best people don't abuse alcohol. They abuse their lives. . . . You're successful, so good things happen. You complete a project, and you feel dynamite. That feeling doesn't last forever, and you slide back to normal. You think, "I've got to start a new project"—which is still normal. But you love the feeling of euphoria, so you've got to have it again. The problem is, you can't stay on that high. Say you're working on a deal and it doesn't get approved. Your self-esteem is on the line, because you've been gathering your self-worth externally. Eventually, in this cycle, you drop to the pain level more and more often. The highs don't seem quite so high. You may win a deal that's even bigger than the one that got away, but somehow that deal doesn't take you to euphoria. Next time, you don't even get back to normal, because you're so desperate about clinching the next deal. . . . An "achievement addict" is no different from any other kind of addict.[54]

In the end, achievement can't really answer the big questions—Who am I? What am I really worth? How do I face death? It gives the initial illusion of an answer. There is an initial rush of happiness that leads us to believe we have arrived, been included, been accepted, and proved ourselves. However, the satisfaction quickly fades.

The Idolatry of Success

More than other idols, personal success and achievement lead to a sense that we ourselves are god, that our security and value rest in our own wisdom, strength, and performance. To be the very best at what you do, to be at the top of the heap, means no one is like you. You are supreme.

One sign that you have made success an idol is the false sense of security it brings. The poor and the marginalized expect suffering, they know that life on this earth is "nasty, brutish, and short." Successful people are much more shocked and overwhelmed by troubles. As a pastor, I've often heard people from the upper echelons say, "Life isn't supposed to be this way," when they face tragedy. I have never heard such language in my years as a pastor among the working class and the poor. The false sense of security comes from deifying our achievement and expecting it to keep us safe from the troubles of life in a way that only God can.

Another sign that you have made achievement an idol is that it distorts your view of yourself. When your achievements serve as the basis for your very worth as a person, they can lead to an inflated view of your abilities. A journalist once told me that she was at a dinner party with a highly successful and wealthy businessman. He dominated the conversation all evening, but the reporter noticed that almost none of the discussion was about economics and finance, his only field of expertise. When he held forth on interior design or single-sex schools or philosophy he acted as if his opinions were equally well informed and authoritative. If your success is more than just success to you—if it is the measure of your value and worth—then accomplishment in one limited area of life will make you believe you have expertise in all areas. This, of course, leads to all kinds of bad choices and decisions. This distorted view of ourselves is part of the blindness to reality that the Bible says always accompanies idolatry (Psalm 135:15–18; Ezekiel 36:22–36).[55]

The main sign that we are into success idolatry, however, is that we find we cannot maintain our self-confidence in life unless we remain at the top of our chosen field. Chris Evert was a leading tennis player in the 1970s and 1980s. Her career win-loss record was the best of any singles player in history. But as she contemplated retirement, she was petrified. She said to an interviewer:

> I had no idea who I was, or what I could be away from tennis. I was depressed and afraid because so much of my life had been defined by my being a tennis champion. I was completely lost. Winning made me feel like I was somebody. It made me feel pretty. It was like being hooked on a drug. I needed the wins, the applause, in order to have an identity.[56]

A friend of mine had reached the top of his profession, but an addiction to prescription drugs forced him to resign his position and enter a period of rehabilitation for substance abuse. He had become addicted in part because of the expectation that he should always be productive, dynamic, upbeat, and brilliant. But he refused to blame other people's demands for his collapse. "My life was built on two premises," he said. "The first was that I could control your opinion and approval of me through my performance. The second was—*that* was all that mattered in life."

It would be wrong for us to think that this idolatry applies only to individuals. It is also possible for an entire field of professionals to be so enamored of their skills and policies that they treat them as a form of salvation. Do scientists, sociologists, therapists, and politicians admit the limitations of what they can accomplish, or do they make "messianic" claims? There should be a chastened humility about how much any public policy or technological advance can do to solve the problems of the human race.

A Culture of Competition

Our contemporary culture makes us particularly vulnerable to turning success into a counterfeit god. In his book *The Homeless Mind,* Peter Berger points out that in traditional cultures, personal worth is measured in terms of "honor." Honor is given to those who fulfill their assigned role in the community, whether it be as citizen, father, mother, teacher, or ruler. Modern society, however, is individualistic, and bases worth on "dignity." Dignity means the right of every individual to develop his or her own identity and self, free from any socially assigned role or category.[57] Modern society, then, puts great pressure on individuals to prove their worth through personal achievement. It is not enough to be a good citizen or family member. You must win, be on top, to show you are one of the best.

David Brooks's book *On Paradise Drive* describes

what he calls "the professionalization of childhood." From the earliest years, an alliance of parents and schools creates a pressure cooker of competition, designed to produce students who excel in everything. Brooks calls this "a massive organic apparatus . . . a mighty Achievatron." The family is no longer what Christopher Lasch once called a "haven in a heartless world," a counterbalance to the dog-eat-dog areas of life.[58] Instead, the family has become the nursery where the craving for success is first cultivated.

This profound emphasis on high achievement is taking a great toll on young people. In spring of 2009, Nathan Hatch, president of Wake Forest University, admitted what many educators have seen for years, that a disproportionate number of young adults have been trying to cram into the fields of finance, consulting, corporate law, and specialized medicine because of the high salaries and aura of success that these professions now bring. Students were doing so with little reference to the larger questions of meaning and purpose, said Hatch. That is, they choose professions not in answer to the question "What job helps people to flourish?" but "What job will help *me* to flourish?" As a result, there is a high degree of frustration expressed over unfulfilling work. Hatch hoped that the economic downturn of 2008–2009 would force many students to reassess their fundamental way of choosing their careers.[59]

If our entire culture strongly encourages us to adopt this counterfeit god, how can we escape it?

The Successful Dead Man

One of the most successful and powerful men in the world in his time was Naaman, whose story is told in the Bible, in 2 Kings 5. Naaman had what some might call "a designer life." He was commander of the army of Aram, which today we call Syria. He was also the equivalent of the prime minister of the nation, since the king of Syria "leaned on his arm" at formal state occasions (2 Kings 5:18). He was a wealthy man and a valiant soldier, highly decorated and honored. However, all of these great accomplishments and abilities had met their match.

> *Naaman was commander of the army of the king of Aram. He was a great man in the sight of his master and highly regarded, because through him the LORD had given victory to Aram. He was a valiant soldier, but he had leprosy.*
>
> 2 Kings 5:1

Notice how the author of 2 Kings piles up the accolades and accomplishments, and suddenly adds that, despite all of them, he was a dead man walking. *Lep-*

rosy in the Bible encompassed a variety of fatal, wasting skin diseases that slowly crippled, disfigured, and finally killed their victims. The word had the resonance in its day that *cancer* has in ours. Naaman's body was going through a slow-motion explosion. His body would puff up, his skin and bones would crack, and then they would fall off in stages as he died by inches. Naaman had everything—wealth, athletic prowess, popular acclaim—but under it all he was literally falling apart.

One of the main motivations behind the drive for success is the hope of entering the "Inner Ring." C. S. Lewis wrote insightfully about this subject in one of his most famous essays.

> I don't believe the economic motive and the erotic motive account for everything that goes on in the world. It's a lust . . . a longing to be inside, [which] takes many forms. . . . You want . . . the delicious knowledge that just we four or five—we are the people who (really) *know.* . . . As long as you are governed by that desire you will never be satisfied. Until you conquer the fear of being an outsider, an outsider you will remain. . . .

What does Lewis mean—"an outsider you will remain"? Naaman had success and money and power, but he was a leper. Success, wealth, and power are supposed to make you the consummate *in*sider, admitted to the most exclusive social circles and inner rings. However, his contagious skin disease had made him an outsider. All his success was useless, since it could not overcome his social alienation and emotional despair.

In this, the story of Naaman functions as a parable. Many people pursue success as a way to overcome the sense that they are somehow "outsiders." If they attain it, they believe, it will open the doors into the clubs, into the social sets, into relationships with the connected and the influential. Finally, they think, they will be accepted by all the people who really matter. Success promises to do that, but in the end it cannot deliver. Naaman's leprosy represents the reality that success can't deliver the satisfaction we are looking for. Many of the most successful people testify to still feeling like "outsiders" and having doubts about themselves.

Looking in the Wrong Places

Now bands from Aram had gone out and had taken captive a young girl from Israel, and she served Naaman's wife. She said to her mistress, "If only my master would see the prophet who is in Samaria! He would cure him of his leprosy."

2 Kings 5:2–3

Naaman's wife had a slave girl who told him about a great prophet in Israel. Desperate enough to grasp at this straw, Naaman set off to Israel, seeking a cure from Elisha. With him he took "ten talents of silver, six thousand shekels of gold, and ten sets of clothing" as well as a letter of reference from the king of Syria to the king of Israel, which read, "With this letter I am sending my servant Naaman to you so that you may cure him of his leprosy" (2 Kings 5:5–6). He immediately headed to the king of Israel, giving him the letter and offering him the money. He expected that, because of the wealth and the letter, the king of Israel would command the prophet to cure him, and he could go home a healthy man.

Naaman expected to get his cure through letters of high recommendation from one king to another king. He thought he could use his success to deal with his problems. Naaman did not understand that there are some things only God can do. The slave girl had told Naaman to simply "see the prophet in Israel," to go directly to the prophet and ask for a cure. This did not fit Naaman's view of the world. Instead he amassed an enormous payout, brought a letter of recommendation from the highest possible source, and went to the top man in Israel, the king. The king of Israel, however, was not pleased.

As soon as the king of Israel read the letter, he tore his robes and said, "Am I God? Can I kill and bring back to life? Why does this fellow send someone to me to be cured of his leprosy? See how he is trying to pick a quarrel with me!"

2 Kings 5:7

Naaman and the Syrian king believed that religion in Israel functioned the way it worked in virtually all nations at that time, and in many nations today. They believed religion was a form of social control. The operating principle of religion is: If you live a good life, then the gods or God will have to bless you and give you prosperity. It was only natural, then, to assume that the most successful people in a society were those closest to God. They would be the ones who could get whatever they wanted from God. That is why traditional religion always expects that the gods will be working through the successful, not the outsider and the failures. That is why Naaman went directly to the king.

The king of Israel, however, tears his clothes when he reads the letter. He knows that the Syrian king will not understand that Israel's God is different and that he cannot command a healing for Naaman. The God of Israel is not on a leash, he cannot be bought or appeased. The gods of religion can be controlled. If we offer them hard work and devotion, then they are beholden to us. However, the God of Israel cannot be approached like that. Whatever he gives us is a gift of grace.

When the king of Israel cried out, "Am I God? Can I kill and bring to life?" he was getting at the heart of Naaman's problem. Naaman had made success an idol. He expected that on the basis of his achievement, he could go to others in his "success-class" and get whatever he needed. But achievement, money, and power cannot "kill and make alive."

The more I have studied this text over the years, the more I admire Naaman. He really was a good and accomplished person. But that only goes to show that the finest person in the world hasn't the slightest idea how to search for God. Let's not be too hard on him. He pulls strings, drops names, spends a lot of money, and goes to the top. This is the way you deal with all important human beings, so why not deal with God this way? But the God of the Bible is not like that. Naaman is after a tame God, but this is a wild God. Naaman is after a God who can be put into debt, but this is a God of grace, who puts everyone else in his debt. Naaman is after a private God, a God for you and you but not a God for everybody, but this God is the God of everyone, whether we acknowledge it or not.

Some Great Thing

When Elisha the man of God heard that the king of Israel had torn his robes, he sent him this message: "Why have you torn your robes? Have the man come to me and he will know that there is a prophet in Israel." So Naaman went with his horses and chariots and stopped at the door of Elisha's house.

2 Kings 5:8–9

Naaman went to the house of Elisha, and what he saw and heard there shocked him. Apparently insensible of the honor being done him, the prophet did not even come to the door. He merely sent his servant to speak with Naaman. The second shock was the message itself.

[The messenger said,] "Go, wash yourself seven times in the Jordan, and your flesh will be restored and you will be cleansed." But Naaman went away angry and said, "I thought that he would surely come out to me and stand and call on the name of the LORD his God, wave his hand over the spot and cure me of my leprosy. Are not Abana and Pharpar, the rivers of Damascus, better than any of the waters of Israel? Couldn't I wash in them and be cleansed?" So he turned and went off

in a rage. Naaman's servants went to him and said, "My father, if the prophet had told you to do some great thing, would you not have done it? How much more, then, when he tells you, 'Wash and be cleansed'!"

2 Kings 5:10–13

Naaman expected that Elisha would take the money and perform some magic ritual. Or, he thought, if Elisha did not take the money, he would at least demand that Naaman do "some great thing" to earn his healing. Instead he was asked to simply go and dip himself seven times in the Jordan River. At this he went off in a rage.

Why? Again, Naaman's entire worldview was being challenged. He had just learned that this God is not an extension of culture, but a transformer of culture, not a controllable but a sovereign Lord. Now he was being confronted with a God who in his dealings with human beings only operates on the basis of grace. These two go together. No one can control the true God because no one can earn, merit, or achieve their own blessing and salvation. Naaman was angry because he thought he was going to be asked to do a mighty thing, as it were; to bring back the broomstick of the Wicked Witch of the West, or to return the Ring of Power to Mount Doom. Those would have been requests in keeping with his self-image and worldview. But Elisha's message was an insult. "Any idiot, any child, anyone can go down and paddle around in the Jordan," he thought to himself. "That takes no ability or attainment *at all*!" Exactly. That is a salvation for anyone, good or bad, weak or strong.

Until Naaman learned that God was a God of grace, whose salvation cannot be earned, only received, he would continue to be enslaved to his idols. He would continue to use them to earn a security and significance that they could not produce. Only if he understood God's grace would he see his successes were ultimately gifts from God. Yes, Naaman had expended much energy to procure them, but only with talents, abilities, and opportunities that God had given to him. He had been dependent on God's grace all his life, but he didn't see it.

"Just wash yourself," then, was a command that was hard because it was so easy. To do it, Naaman had to admit he was helpless and weak and had to receive his salvation as a free gift. If you want God's grace, all you need is need, all you need is nothing. But that kind of spiritual humility is hard to muster. We come to God saying, "Look at all I've done," or maybe "Look at all I've suffered." God, however, wants us to look to him—to just wash.

Naaman needed to learn how to "lay his deadly doing down." That phrase comes from an old hymn:

> *Lay your deadly "doing" down*
> *Down at Jesus' feet.*
> *Stand in him, in him alone,*
> *Gloriously complete.*

The Little Suffering Servant

At every point in the Bible, the writers are at pains to stress that God's grace and forgiveness, while free to the recipient, are always costly for the giver. From the earliest parts of the Bible, it was understood that God could not forgive without sacrifice. No one who is seriously wronged can "just forgive" the perpetrator. If you have been robbed of money, opportunity, or happiness, you can either make the wrongdoer pay it back or you can forgive. But when you forgive, that means *you* absorb the loss and the debt. You bear it yourself. All forgiveness, then, is costly.[60]

It is remarkable how often the biblical narratives make reference to this basic principle. In this story, too, someone had to bear her suffering with patience and love, in order for Naaman to receive his blessing. I'm referring to a character in the narrative who entered and exited so quickly that she is hardly noticed. Yet she was in some ways the most important character in the story. Who was she? The slave girl of Naaman's wife was captured by raiding bands of Syrians. At best that meant her family was taken captive and all sold off. At worst, it meant they had been killed before her eyes. When we meet her in the story, she's at the bottom of the bottom of Syria's social structure. She's a racial outsider, a slave, a woman—and a young one, probably aged twelve to fourteen. In short, her life has been ruined utterly. And who is responsible? Field Marshal Naaman, the supreme military commander. Yet how does she respond when she learns that her nemesis has been struck down with leprosy?

If we set our hearts on getting to the top, but instead find ourselves on the bottom rung of the ladder, it will usually lead to great cynicism and bitterness. We will desperately look around for people to blame for our failures. We might even indulge in fantasies of revenge. However, the little slave girl did not fall into that trap. Did she say, "Ha! Leprosy! I saw another finger fall off today! Oh, I will dance on his grave!" No, not at all. Look at her words—"If only my master would see the prophet!" There is sympathy and concern in those words. She must have really wanted to relieve his suffering and save him. There was no other reason to tell him about the prophet. Think of it. He was now in her hands. What she knew could save him, and by withholding it she could make him suffer horribly. She could have made him pay for his sins. She could have made *him* bear the cost for what he had done to her. He had abused her, and now she could abuse him.

However, she did not do that. This unsung heroine of the Bible refused to relieve her own suffering by making him pay. She did what the entire Bible tells us to do. She did not seek revenge, she trusted God to be the judge of all. She forgave him and became the vehicle for his healing and salvation. She trusted God and bore her suffering with patience. As the British preacher Dick Lucas once said about her, "She paid the price of usefulness." She suffered and forgave not knowing how much God would use her sacrifice.[61]

The Great Suffering Servant

This biblical theme, that forgiveness always requires a suffering servant, finds its climax in Jesus, who fulfills the prophecies of a Suffering Servant who will come to save the world (Isaiah 53). Though he had lived in joy and glory with his father, he lost it all. He became a human being, a servant, and was subject to beatings, capture, and death. As he looked down from the

Cross at his so-called friends, with some of them denying, some betraying, and all forsaking him, he paid the price. He forgave them and died on the Cross for them. On the Cross we see God doing at the cosmic level what we all have to do when we forgive. There God absorbed the punishment and debt for sin himself. He paid it so we did not have to.

We will not escape our idolatry of success simply by berating ourselves over it. At the end of the 1990s, just before the dot-com crash and September 11, 2001, the excessive emphasis on success and materialism was exposed in an article by Helen Rubin in the magazine *Fast Company*.

> Of all the subjects we obsess about . . . success is the one we lie about the most—that success and its cousin money will make us secure, that success and its cousin power will make us important, that success and its cousin fame will make us happy. It's time to tell the truth: Why are our generation's smartest, most talented, most successful people flirting with disaster in record numbers? People are using all their means to get money, power, and glory—and then self-destructing. Maybe they didn't want it in the first place! Or didn't like what they saw when they finally achieved it.[62]

The Seduction of Success

Not long after this article was written, in light of the mild recession of 2000–2001, there were many similar jeremiads about how our culture had become addicted to success. When would we learn that we have made success and its "cousins" into the gods of our society? Then the attacks of September 11, 2001, occurred and the media announced the "end of irony." Now, it was said, we would go back to more traditional values of hard work, modest expectations, and delayed gratification. Nothing like that happened. In 2008–2009, when the global economy crashed, it became clear that our culture had gone back to its addiction.

The idol of success cannot be just expelled, it must be replaced. The human heart's desire for a particular valuable object may be conquered, but its need to have *some* such object is unconquerable.[63] How can we break our heart's fixation on doing "some great thing" in order to heal ourselves of our sense of inadequacy, in order to give our lives meaning? Only when we see what Jesus, our great Suffering Servant, has done for us will we finally understand why God's salvation does not require us to do "some great thing." We don't have to do it, because Jesus has. That's why we can "just wash." Jesus did it all for us, and he loves us—that is how we know our existence is justified. When we believe in what he accomplished for us with our minds, and when we are moved by what he did for us in our hearts, it begins to kill off the addiction, the need for success at all costs.

The End of Idolatry

Naaman humbled himself and went to the Jordan. The results were astonishing.

> *So he went down and dipped himself in the Jordan seven times, as the man of God had told him, and his flesh was restored and became clean like that of a young boy. Then Naaman and all his attendants went back to the man of God. He stood before him and said, "Now I know that there is no God in all the world except in Israel. Please accept now a gift from your servant." The prophet answered, "As surely as the LORD lives, whom I serve, I will not accept a thing." And even though Naaman urged him, he refused.*
>
> 2 Kings 5:14–16

The biblical story of salvation assaults our worship of success at every point. Naaman, to be cured, had to accept a word through a servant girl, and later through a servant of Elisha, and finally other servants of his own. In those days such people were treated as no more important than a pet or a beast of burden by the high and mighty. Yet God sent his message of salvation through them. The answer came not from the palace, but from the slave quarters! The ultimate example of this theme, of course, is Jesus Christ himself. He came not to Rome or Alexandria or to China, but to a backwater colony. He was born not in the palace, but in a manger, in a stable.

> *Seek not in courts nor palaces*
> *Nor royal curtains draw—*
> *But search the stable, see your God*
> *Extended on the straw.*

> —William Billings

All during his ministry, the disciples continually asked Jesus, "When are you going to take power? When are you going to stop fraternizing with simple people? When are you going to start networking and raising money? When will you run for office? When's the first primary? When's our first TV special?" Instead, Jesus served humbly and then was tortured and killed. Even when Jesus rose from the dead he first appeared to women, the people who then had no status. Jesus's salvation is received not through strength but through the admission of weakness and need. And Jesus's salvation was achieved not through strength but through surrender, service, sacrifice, and death. This is one of the great messages of the Bible: God chooses the weak things of the world to shame the strong, the foolish and despised things to shame the wise, even the things that are not, to bring to nothing the things that are (1 Corinthians 1:29-31). That's how God does it.

FIVE

THE POWER AND THE GLORY

A World Possessed

Just before Europe plunged into World War II, Dutch historian Johan Huizinga wrote, "We live in a world possessed. And we know it."[64] The Nazis claimed to promote deep love of country and people. But somehow as they pursued this thing, "love of country," their patriotism became demonic and destructive. In the end, Nazism accomplished the very opposite of what it sought—endless shame rather than national honor.

In 1794, Maximilien Robespierre, the leader of the French Revolution, said to the National Convention, "What is the goal towards which we are heading? The peaceful enjoyment of liberty and equality. . . . The Terror is nothing other than prompt, severe, inflexible justice."[65] However, his "Reign of Terror" was so horrendously *un*just that Robespierre himself was made a scapegoat and guillotined without any trial. "Liberty and equality" are obviously great goods, but again, something went horribly wrong. A noble principle became "possessed," went insane, and ultimately accomplished the very opposite of the justice the revolutionaries sought.

What happened? Idolatry. When love of one's people becomes an absolute, it turns into racism. When love of equality turns into a supreme thing, it can result in hatred and violence toward anyone who has led a privileged life. It is the settled tendency of human societies to turn good political causes into counterfeit gods. As we have mentioned, Ernest Becker wrote that in a society that has lost the reality of God, many people will look to romantic love to give them the fulfillment they once found in religious experience. Nietzsche, however, believed it would be money that would replace God. But there is another candidate to fill this spiritual vacuum. We can also look to politics. We can look upon our political leaders as "messiahs," our political policies as saving doctrine, and turn our political activism into a kind of religion.

The Signs of Political Idolatry

One of the signs that an object is functioning as an idol is that fear becomes one of the chief characteristics of life. When we center our lives on the idol, we become dependent on it. If our counterfeit god is threatened in any way, our response is complete panic. We do not say, "What a shame, how difficult," but rather "This is the end! There's no hope!"

This may be a reason why so many people now respond to U.S. political trends in such an extreme way. When either party wins an election, a certain percentage of the losing side talks openly about leaving the country. They become agitated and fearful for the future. They have put the kind of hope in their political leaders and policies that once was reserved for God and the work of the gospel. When their political leaders are out of power, they experience a death. They believe that if *their* policies and people are not in power, everything will fall apart. They refuse to admit how much agreement they actually have with the other party, and instead focus on the points of disagreement. The points of contention overshadow everything else, and a poisonous environment is created.

Another sign of idolatry in our politics is that opponents are not considered to be simply mistaken, but to be evil. After the last presidential election, my eighty-four-year-old mother observed, "It used to be that whoever was elected as your president, even if he wasn't the one you voted for, he was still your president. That doesn't seem to be the case any longer." After each election, there is now a significant number of people who see the incoming president lacking moral legitimacy. The increasing political polarization and bitterness we see in U.S. politics today is a sign that we have made political activism into a form of religion. How does idolatry produce fear and demonization?

Dutch-Canadian philosopher Al Wolters taught that in the biblical view of things, the main problem in life is sin, and the only solution is God and his grace. The alternative to this view is to identify something besides sin as the main problem with the world and something besides God as the main remedy. That demonizes something that is not completely bad, and makes an idol out of something that cannot be the ultimate good. Wolters writes:

> The great danger is to single out some aspect or phenomenon of God's good creation and identify it, rather than the alien intrusion of sin, as the villain in the drama of human life. . . . This "something" has been variously identified as . . . the body and its passions (Plato and much of Greek philosophy), culture in distinction from nature (Rousseau and Romanticism), institutional authority, especially in the state and the family (much of depth psychology), technology and management techniques (Heidegger and Ellul). . . . The Bible is unique in its uncompromising rejection

of all attempts to . . . identify part of creation as either the villain or the savior.[66]

This accounts for the constant political cycles of overblown hopes and disillusionment, for the increasingly poisonous political discourse, and for the disproportionate fear and despair when one's political party loses power. But *why* do we deify and demonize political causes and ideas? Reinhold Niebuhr answered that, in political idolatry, we make a god out of having power.

The Idolatry of Power

Reinhold Niebuhr was a prominent American theologian of the mid-twentieth century. He believed all humans struggle with a sense of being dependent and powerless. The original temptation in the Garden of Eden was to resent the limits God had put on us ("You shall not eat of the tree. . . ."; Genesis 2:17) and to seek to be "as God" by taking power over our own destiny. We gave in to this temptation and now it is part of our nature. Rather than accept our finitude and dependence on God, we desperately seek ways to assure ourselves that we still have power over our own lives. But this is an illusion. Niebuhr believed this cosmic insecurity creates a "will to power" that dominates our social and political relationships.[67] He observed two ways this works itself out.

First, said Niebuhr, pride in one's people is a good thing, but when the power and prosperity of the nation become unconditioned absolutes that veto all other concerns, then violence and injustice can be perpetrated without question.[68] When this happens, Dutch scholar Bob Goudzwaard writes:

> . . . the end indiscriminately justifies every means. . . . Thus a nation's goal of material prosperity becomes an idol when we use it to justify the destruction of the natural environment or allow the abuse of individuals or classes of people. A nation's goal of military security becomes an idol when we use it to justify the removal of rights to free speech and judicial process, or the abuse of an ethnic minority.[69]

Niebuhr believed that entire nations had corporate "egos," and just as individuals, national cultures could have both superiority and inferiority complexes. An example of the former would be how America's proud self-image as "the land of the free" blinded most people to their hypocritical racism toward African-Americans. A society can also develop a sense of inferiority and become aggressive and belligerent. Writing his book in 1941, it was easy for Niebuhr to identify Nazi Germany as an example of this form of power idolatry. Germany's humiliation after World War I left the whole society eager to prove its power and superiority to the world.[70]

It is not easy to draw an exact line between ascribing value to something and assigning it absolute value. There is likewise no precise way to define when patriotism has crossed over into racism, oppression, and imperialism. Yet no one denies that nations have often slid down that slippery slope. It is no solution to laugh at all expressions of patriotism, as if it were an evil thing in itself. As we have seen all along, idols are good and necessary things that are turned into gods. C. S. Lewis wrote wisely about this:

> It is a mistake to think that some of our impulses—say mother love or patriotism—are good, and others, like sex or the fighting instinct, are bad. . . . There are situations in which it is the duty of a married man to encourage his sexual impulse and of a soldier to encourage the fighting instinct. There are also occasions on which a mother's love for her own children or a man's love for his own country have to be suppressed or they will lead to unfairness towards other people's children or countries.[71]

Turning a Philosophy into an Idol

Niebuhr recognized another form of the "will to power." You make not your people, but your political philosophy into a saving faith. This happens when politics becomes "ideological."

Ideology can be used to refer to any coherent set of ideas about a subject, but it can also have a negative connotation closer to its cousin word, *idolatry*. An ideology, like an idol, is a limited, partial account of reality that is raised to the level of the final word on things. Ideologues believe that their school or party has the real and complete answer to society's problems. Above all, ideologies hide from their adherents their dependence on God.[72]

The most recent example of a major ideology that failed is communism. For nearly a hundred years, large numbers of Western thinkers had high hopes for what once was called "scientific socialism." But from the end of World War II to the fall of the Berlin Wall in 1989, those beliefs came crashing down. C. E. M. Joad was a leading British agnostic philosopher who turned back to Christianity after World War II. In his book *The Recovery of Belief* he wrote:

The view of evil implied by Marxism, expressed by Shaw and maintained by modern psychotherapy, a view which regards evil as the by-product of circumstances, which circumstances can, therefore, alter and even eliminate, has come to seem [in light of World War II and atrocities by both Nazis and Stalinists] intolerably shallow. . . . It was because we rejected the doctrine of original sin that we on the Left were always being disappointed, disappointed . . . by the failure of true socialism to arrive, by the behavior of nations and politicians . . . above all, by the recurrent fact of war.[73]

One of the key volumes that came out of this time was a book by several disillusioned communists and socialists, including Arthur Koestler and André Gide, entitled *The God that Failed*.[74] The title says it all, describing how a political ideology can make absolute promises and demand total life commitment.

In the wake of the collapse of socialism, the pendulum swung toward an embrace of free market capitalism as the best solution for dealing with the recurrent problems of poverty and injustice. Many would say today that this is the new reigning ideology. Indeed, one of the source documents of modern capitalism, Adam Smith's *The Wealth of Nations,* seemed to deify the free market when it argued that the market is an "invisible hand" that, when given free rein, automatically drives human behavior toward that which is most beneficial for society, apart from any dependence on God or a moral code.[75] It is too early to be sure, but it may be that in light of the massive financial crisis of 2008–2009, the same disaffection with capitalism may occur that happened to socialism a generation before. A wave of books revealing the ideological nature of recent market capitalism, both popular[76] and scholarly,[77] both secular[78] and religious,[79] is appearing. Some even have variants on the title "the god that failed," since free markets have been ascribed a godlike power to make us happy and free.[80]

Niebuhr argued that human thinking always elevates *some* finite value or object to be The Answer.[81] That way we feel that we are the people who can fix things, that everyone opposing us is a fool or evil. But as with all idolatries, this too blinds us. In Marxism the powerful State becomes the savior and capitalists are demonized. In conservative economic thought, free markets and competition will solve our problems, and therefore liberals and government are the obstacles to a happy society.

The reality is much less simplistic. Highly progressive tax structures can produce a kind of injustice where people who have worked hard go unrewarded and are penalized by the high taxes. A society of low taxes and few benefits, however, produces a different kind of injustice, where the children of families who can afford good health care and elite education have vastly better opportunities than those who cannot. In short, ideologues cannot admit that there are always significant negative side-effects to *any* political program. They cannot grant that their opponents have good ideas too.

In any culture in which God is largely absent, sex, money, and politics will fill the vacuum for different people. This is the reason that our political discourse is increasingly ideological and polarized. Many describe the current poisonous public discourse as a lack of bi-partisanship, but the roots go much deeper than that. As Niebuhr taught, they go back to the beginning of the world, to our alienation from God, and to our frantic efforts to compensate for our feelings of cosmic nakedness and powerlessness. The only way to deal with all these things is to heal our relationship with God.

The Bible gives us a dramatic example of such a healing. It is the story of a man whose will to dominance drove him to become the most powerful man in the world.

The Insecure King

In the sixth century before Christ, the Babylonian empire rose to displace Assyria and Egypt as the dominant world power. Soon it invaded Judah and captured Jerusalem, exiling Israel's professional class, including military officers, artists, and scholars, to Babylon. Eventually most of the known world was under the sway of Babylon's king and general, Nebuchadnezzar. In the biblical book of Daniel, chapter 2, however, we learn that the most powerful man on earth slept uneasily.

> *In the second year of his reign, Nebuchadnezzar had dreams; his mind was troubled and he could not sleep. So the king summoned the magicians, enchanters, sorcerers and astrologers to tell him what he had dreamed. When they came in and stood before the king, he said to them, "I have had a dream that troubles me and I want to know what it means."*
>
> Daniel 2:1–3

Nebuchadnezzar was deeply troubled by the dream. His dream had been about a towering figure, and it may be that this is the vision he wanted the world to have of him—"an impregnable giant, towering over the world. . . ."[82] However, the statue had "feet of clay" and came crashing down. He woke up in a sweat. Did this mean his empire would fail? Or that someone would come and exploit hidden weaknesses?

Many people with a great drive for power are very anxious and fearful. Niebuhr believed that fear and anxiety are the reason that many seek political power.[83] However, even if fear is not a reason for seeking power, it almost always comes with having it. Those in power know that they are the object of jealousy and stand in the crosshairs of their competitors. The higher a person climbs the greater the possibility of a terrible fall, for there is now so much to lose. When Bernard Madoff was sentenced to 150 years in prison for running a $65 billion Ponzi scheme, he publicly blamed his pride. At some time in the past he had faced a year in which he should have reported significant losses, but he could not "admit his failures as a money manager."[84] He could not accept the loss of power and reputation that such an admission would bring. Once he began to hide his weaknesses through the Ponzi scheme, he then "couldn't admit his error in judgment while the scheme grew," always thinking he could "work his way out."[85]

Power, then, is often born of fear and in turn gives birth to more fear. The dream was forcing Nebuchadnezzer's insecurity to the surface, and it was exceedingly uncomfortable. Powerful people do not like to admit how weak they really feel.

The Fear of Powerlessness

Nebuchadnezzar is a classic case study of what Niebuhr says about sin, politics, and power in *The Nature and Destiny of Man.* In the chapter "Man as Sinner" Niebuhr argues that "man is insecure, and . . . he seeks to overcome his insecurity by a will-to-power. . . . He pretends he is not limited."[86] Human beings have very little real power over their lives. Ninety-five percent of what sets the course of their lives is completely outside their control. This includes the century and place they are born in, who their parents and family are, their childhood environment, physical stature, genetically hardwired talents, and most of the circumstances that they find themselves in. In short, all we are and have is given to us by God. We are not infinite Creators, but finite, dependent creatures.

The British poet W. E. Henley had a leg amputated as a teenager. Yet he went on to have a career as a critic and author. As a young man Henley defiantly penned the famous "Invictus," Latin for "unconquered."

> *It matters not how strait the gate,*
> *How charged with punishments the scroll,*
> *I am the master of my fate:*
> *I am the captain of my soul.*

As Niebuhr points out, this is an enormous exaggeration, a view of reality distorted and "infected with the sin of pride."[87] No one wants to minimize the importance of learning to overcome obstacles in one's life, but Henley's success would have been impossible had he been born without literary talent, with below-average IQ, or with different parents and social connections. And, somewhat like Nebuchadnezzar, he was forced to face his own powerlessness when his five-year-old daughter died, a blow from which he never recovered. He was a finite and limited man in a world of indomitable forces.

If Niebuhr is right, and human beings have a deep fear of powerlessness stemming from their alienation from God, then there must be many ways that they deal with it, not just through politics and government. Power idols are a "deep idols" that can express themselves through a great variety of other "surface" idols.[88]

During my college years I knew a man who, before professing faith in Christ, was a notorious womanizer. James's pattern was to seduce a woman and, once he had sex with her, lose interest and move on. When he embraced Christianity he quickly renounced his sexual escapades. He became active in Christian ministry. However, his deep idol did not change. In every class or study, James was argumentative and dominating. In every meeting he had to be the leader, even if he was not designated to be so. He was abrasive and harsh with skeptics when talking to them about his new-found faith. Eventually it became clear that his meaning and value had not shifted to Christ, but was still based in having power over others. That is what made him feel alive. The reason James wanted to have sex with those women was not because he was attracted to them, but because he was seeking the power of knowing he could sleep with them if he wanted to. Once he achieved that power, he lost interest in them. The reason he wanted to be in Christian ministry was not because he was attracted to serving God and others, but to the power of knowing he was right, that he had the truth. His power idol took a sexual form, and then a religious one. It hid itself well.

Idols of power, then, are not only for the powerful. You can pursue power in small, petty ways, by becoming a local neighborhood bully or a low-level bureaucrat who bosses around the few people in his field of authority. Power idolatry is all around us. What is the cure?

The Chastened King

Nebuchadnezzar's wise men could not interpret his dream for him. Finally, a court official who was one of the Jewish exiles, named Daniel, came forward. By God's power he was able to tell the king the content of his dream, even though Nebuchadnezzar had yet to reveal it. Then he went on to interpret it.

"You looked, O king, and there before you stood a large statue—an enormous, dazzling statue, awesome in appearance. The head of the statue was made of pure gold, its chest and arms of silver, its belly and thighs of bronze, its legs of iron, its feet partly of iron and partly of baked clay. While you watched, a rock was cut out, but not by human hands. It struck the statue on its feet of iron and clay and smashed them. Then the iron, the clay, the bronze, the silver and the gold were broken to pieces at the same time and became like chaff on a threshing floor in the summer. The wind swept them away without leaving a trace. But the rock that struck the statue became a huge mountain and filled the whole earth."

Daniel 2:31–35

The statue represented the kingdoms of the earth. It appeared as a giant idol, and represented the idolization of human power and achievement. It was human civilization—commerce and culture, rule and power, all exercised by human beings to glorify themselves. What smashed the idol was a stone. In contrast to the rest of the materials in the statue it was "cut out, not by human hands." It was from God. Though the stone was less valuable than any of the metals in the statue, it was ultimately the most powerful component. It was, as Daniel says, God's kingdom (Verse 44) that would someday be set up on the earth.

The dream was a call to humility. Though circumstances often appear to favor tyrants, God will eventually bring them down, whether gradually or dramatically.[89] Those in power should see that they have not achieved power but have only been given it by God, and that all human power crumbles in the end.

Nebuchadnezzar was being asked to change his conception of God. As a pagan, he would have believed in pluralism, that there are many gods and supernatural forces in the world. He had not believed, however, that there was one preeminent, all-powerful lawgiver to whom everyone was accountable, including him. He was being told that there was one supreme God, who was sovereign and judge, and to whom he was responsible for his use of power.

Nebuchadnezzar accepted the message.

Then King Nebuchadnezzar fell prostrate before Daniel and paid him honor and ordered that an offering and incense be presented to him. The king said to Daniel, "Surely your God is the God of gods and the Lord of kings and a revealer of mysteries, for you were able to reveal this mystery."

Daniel 2:46–47

The king confessed that God is "Lord of kings," and the most powerful man in the world prostrated himself—an act of humility quite out of accord with Nebuchadnezzar's accustomed pride.

The Illusion that We Are in Control

What we learn here is that theology matters, that much of our addiction to power and control is due to false conceptions of God. Gods of our own making may allow us to be "masters of our fate." Sociologist Christian Smith gave the name "moralistic, therapeutic deism" to the dominant understanding of God he discovered among younger Americans. In his book *Soul Searching: The Religious and Spiritual Lives of American Teenagers,* he describes this set of beliefs. God blesses and takes to heaven those who try to live good and decent lives (the "moralistic" belief). The central goal of life is not to sacrifice, or to deny oneself, but to be happy and feel good about yourself (the "therapeutic" belief). Though God exists and created the world, he does not need to be particularly involved in our lives except when there is a problem (that is "deism").[90]

This view of God literally makes you master of your fate and captain of your soul. Salvation and happiness is up to you. Some have pointed out that "moralistic, therapeutic deism" could only develop in a comfortable, prosperous society among privileged people. People "at the top" are eager to attribute their position to their own intellect, savvy, and hard work. The reality is much more complicated. Personal connections, family environment, and what appears to be plain luck determine how successful a person is. We are the product of three things—genetics, environment, and our personal choices—but two of these three factors we have no power over. We are not nearly as responsible for our success as our popular views of God and reality lead us to think.

Popular culture often tells young people, "You can be *any*thing you set your mind to." But it is cruel to say that to a five-foot-four-inch eighteen-year-old boy who yearns, more than anything else, to be an NFL linebacker. To use an extreme example, if you had been born in a yurt in Outer Mongolia, instead of where you were, it wouldn't have mattered how hard you worked or used your talents—you would have ended up poor and powerless. To come closer to home, think of the impact of your family background on you. You may spend your younger years telling yourself that you will *not* be like your parents, you will be your own person. However, somewhere around the middle of your life, it will become clearer how indelibly your family has shaped you.

The Power and the Glory

Malcolm Gladwell's book *Outliers* is filled with case studies that demonstrate how our success is largely the product of our environment. He gives an example of a number of Jewish New York City lawyers, all born about 1930. An "accident of time" gave them many advantages. They went to underpopulated schools where they received more attention from teachers. Extremely high-quality yet inexpensive college and legal educations were open to them at the time. Because of anti-Semitic attitudes, they were excluded from white-shoe law firms, which forced them to go into specializations such as proxy fights that established lawyers would not touch. But it turned out that this gave them enormous competitive advantage in the seventies and eighties when hostile takeovers began. They all made enormous amounts of money.[91] Although, unlike Gladwell, I would grant equal importance to the three factors of heredity, environment, and personal choice, his book makes a strong case that we are not as personally responsible for our success as we would like to think. Most of the forces that make us who we are lie in the hand of God. We should not "take pride in one man over against another," wrote the Apostle Paul. "For who makes you different from anyone else? What do you have that you did not receive? And if you did receive it, why do you boast as though you did not?" (1 Corinthians 4:6–7)

Nebuchadnezzar had taken personal credit for his rise to prominence. Now he began to be humbled, and his false views of God began to change, but the changes didn't go very deep. More intervention by God would be necessary.

The Mad King

In chapter 4 Nebuchadnezzar describes himself as being at home in his palace, contented and prosperous, when he suffered another dream, this one not merely troubling but terrifying. It was a dream about an enormous tree: "Its top touched the sky, it was visible to the ends of the earth. . . . From it every creature was fed" (Daniel 4:11–12). But then a voice was heard, calling to "cut down the tree." And the voice began to talk about the tree, calling it "he," saying, "Let the stump and its roots . . . remain in the ground. . . . Let his mind be changed from that of a man and let him be given the mind of an animal, till seven times pass by for him."

With fear and trembling, the king called for Daniel, who heard the dream and blanched. After standing silent for a time, he gave the interpretation.

This is the interpretation, O king, and this is the decree the Most High has issued against my lord the king: You will be driven away from people and will

*live with the wild animals; you will eat grass like
cattle and be drenched with the dew of heaven. Seven
times will pass by for you until you acknowledge that
the Most High is sovereign over the kingdoms of men
and gives them to anyone he wishes. The command
to leave the stump of the tree with its roots means
that your kingdom will be restored to you when you
acknowledge that Heaven rules. Therefore, O king,
be pleased to accept my advice: Renounce your sins
by doing what is right, and your wickedness by being
kind to the oppressed. It may be that then your prosperity will continue.*

Daniel 4:24–27

The first dream had been, in a sense, an academic
lesson. It spoke in general terms about the character
of God, and the character of human power. This time,
God was getting personal. The academic lessons had
not helped. He was still a tyrant. He still oppressed
particular races, classes, and the poor (Verse 27). Now
God was going to teach him what he needed to learn.
But there was hope. The tree would be cut down, but
the stump would be left in the ground to grow back.
God was not after retribution, vengeance, or destruction. This was discipline—pain inflicted with the mo-
tive of correction and redemption.

What was, then, the lesson that God wanted to drive

into Nebuchadnezzar's heart? It was this: "The Most High is sovereign over the kingdoms of men and gives them to anyone he wishes and sets over them the lowliest of men." This means that anyone who is successful is simply a recipient of God's unmerited favor. Even the people at the top of the world's hierarchy of power, wealth, and influence are really "lowliest"—they are no better than anyone else. This is a rudimentary form of the gospel—that what we have is the result of grace, not of our "works" or efforts.

God was saying something like this: "King Nebuchadnezzar—you must understand that your power has been given to you by grace from God. If you knew that, you would be both more relaxed and secure *and* more humble and just. If you think you earned your position through your own merit and works, you will continue to be both scared and cruel."

> *Twelve months later, as the king was walking on the roof of the royal palace of Babylon, he said, "Is not this the great Babylon I have built as the royal residence, by my mighty power and for the glory of my majesty?"*
>
> Daniel 4:29–30

The king looked over his realm and as he did so the pride of his heart asserted itself. At that moment, a voice from heaven said: "You will be driven away from people and will live with the wild animals; you will eat grass like cattle . . . until you acknowledge that the Most High is sovereign over the kingdoms of men and gives them to anyone he wishes" (Daniel 4:31–32). Immediately, Nebuchadnezzar fell into what apparently was a period of severe mental illness, in which he was too deranged to live inside the palace but lived on palace grounds among the animals.

A Resurrection from the Death of Pride

What happened? One of the great ironies of sin is that when human beings try to become more than human beings, to be as gods, they fall to become lower than human beings. To be your own God and live for your own glory and power leads to the most bestial and cruel kind of behavior. Pride makes you a predator, not a person.[92] That is what happened to the king.

In C. S. Lewis's children's book *The Voyage of the Dawn Treader,* one of the main characters is a young boy named Eustace Scrubb. Eustace clearly had a lust for power, but he expressed it in the mean, petty ways that only a schoolboy could, in teasing, torturing animals, tattling, and ingratiating adult authorities. He was a Nebuchadnezzar-in-training.

One night Eustace found an enormous pile of treasure in a cave. He was elated and began to imagine the life of ease and power he would now have. When he woke, however, to his horror, he had turned into a hideous dragon. "Sleeping on a dragon's hoard with greedy, dragonish thoughts in his heart, he had become a dragon himself."[93]

Becoming a dragon was a "cosmic natural consequence." Because he thought like a dragon, he had become a dragon. When we set our hearts on power, we become hardened predators. We become like what we worship.[94]

Eustace was now an enormously powerful being, far more powerful than he had ever dreamed, but he was also fearful, hideous, and completely lonely. This, of course, is what power for its own sake does to us. The shock of his transformation humbled Eustace and he longed to be a normal boy again. As his pride faded, the idolatry in his heart began to be healed.

One night Eustace the dragon met a mysterious lion. The lion challenged him to "undress," to try to take off his dragon skin. He managed to peel off a layer, but found he was still a dragon underneath. He tried repeatedly but made no further progress. The lion finally said:

"You will have to let me undress you." I was afraid of his claws, I can tell you, but I was pretty nearly desperate now. So I just lay flat down on my back to let him do it. The very first tear he made was so deep that I thought it had gone right into my heart. And when he began pulling the skin off, it hurt worse than anything I've ever felt. . . . Well, he peeled the beastly stuff right off—just as I thought I'd done it myself the other three times, only they hadn't hurt—and there it was lying on the grass: only ever so much thicker, and darker, and more knobbly-looking than the others had been. And there was I as smooth and soft as a peeled switch and smaller than I had been. . . . I'd turned into a boy again.[95]

The lion of the fairy tale, Aslan, represents Christ, and the story bears witness to what all Christians have discovered, that pride leads to death, to breakdown, to a loss of humanity. But if you let it humble you rather than embitter you, and turn to God instead of living for your own glory, then the death of your pride can lead to a resurrection. You can emerge, finally, fully human, with a tender heart instead of a hard heart.

Something like this happened to Nebuchadnezzar. In the words of his own testimony:

At the end of that time, I, Nebuchadnezzar, raised my eyes toward heaven, and my sanity was restored.

*Then I praised the Most High; I honored and glo-
rified him who lives forever. His dominion is an
eternal dominion; his kingdom endures from generation to generation. . . . At the same time that
my sanity was restored, my honor and splendor were
returned to me for the glory of my kingdom. My ad-
visers and nobles sought me out, and I was restored
to my throne and became even greater than before.*

Daniel 4:34, 36

When he "raised his eyes toward heaven," to look
to God, the result was more than the restoration of his
sanity. He had become "greater than before" (Verse
36). This is a deep pattern of grace, which we see supremely in Jesus. Our hearts say, "I will ascend, I will
be as the Most High for my own sake," but Jesus said,
"I will descend, I will go low, for their sakes." He became human and went to the Cross to die for our sins
(Philippians 2:4–10). Jesus *lost* all power and served, in
order to save us. He died, but that led to redemption
and resurrection. So if like Eustace, Nebuchadnezzar,
and Jesus you fall into great weakness, but say, "Father,
into your hands, I commit my spirit" (Luke 23:46),
there will be growth, a change, and a resurrection.

Jesus's example and grace heals our will to power.
The normal response to our sense of powerlessness is
to deny it, to find people to dominate and control in

order to live in that denial. But Jesus shows us another way. By giving up his power and serving, he became the most influential man who ever lived. Jesus is not only an example, however, he is a Savior. Only by admitting our sin, need, and powerlessness, and by casting ourselves on his mercy, will we finally become secure in his love, and therefore empowered in a way that does not lead us to oppress others. The insecurity is gone, the lust for power is cut at the root. As a preacher once said, "The way up is to go down; the way down is to go up."

SIX

The Hidden Idols in Our Lives

So far we have looked at personal idols, such as romantic love, financial prosperity, or political success. These counterfeit gods are not so hard to spot. There are others, however, that influence us but are more hidden. They are not the idols of our heart, but of our culture and society.

The God of Profit

A writer in the *New York Times* Sunday Opinion section recently wrote about a friend named Melissa, a twenty-nine-year-old who was a vice president at J. P. Morgan until recently being laid off. While "just about everyone is still angry at Wall Street . . . Melissa doesn't exactly fit the villainous cliché of the greedy trader who's collecting millions in bonus money while her company burns." She was well-paid but was very generous with her money toward friends and charitable nonprofits. However, her specialty was securitizing subprime mortgages, student loans, and credit card debt. "That all this debt she was putting together like a puzzle and selling to investors would play such a sinister role in the downfall of the economy didn't occur to her—although it probably should have."[96] Why didn't it occur to her? As Nathan Hatch said in Chapter Four, our culture does not equip students to ask those kinds of questions about a job. Usually the only question is—what does it pay?

In an unofficial ceremony the day before they graduated, nearly half of the 2009 class of Harvard Business School promised to "act with the utmost integrity," resist "decisions and behavior that advance my own narrow ambitions," and work in a manner that "enhances the value my enterprise can create for society over the long term."[97] In coverage of this "MBA Oath," *The Economist* evoked Milton Friedman's claim that business managers have one and only one goal—to maximize shareholder value.[98] That, goes the traditional argument, is the only way that a business promotes the common good, by creating jobs and generating new products. The market itself rewards integrity and punishes dishonesty; if you lie or cheat, it will catch up with you and you will lose money. The only goal of business, then, is to maximize profits. All other talk of ethical management or socially conscious business, it was said, is unnecessary.

The signers of the oath begged to differ. Managers in pursuit of profit can do things to run up share price quickly at the expense of the company's long-term health, and also at the expense of the good of its workers, its customers, and the environment. Then they can cash out and leave everyone else poorer. While some argue that paying employees more and giving them a good working environment pays off in greater profits in the long run, that is not self-evident. It should be done because it is a good and right thing to do in and of itself, not only as a means to the end of higher profits.

Also, it is not true to say that honesty and integrity always make for good business. In certain situations doing the honest thing would be financially ruinous, and therefore, according to strict cost-benefit analysis, the risk of getting caught in a lie is clearly worth taking. Things like honesty and commitment to one's workers and environment must be embraced as goods in themselves—equally important as profit—or integrity will not be maintained.

The signers, then, were arguing that profit had become a counterfeit god—a good thing turned into an absolute value. The result has been moral and social breakdown. Their oath was an effort to take on a cultural idol that has had a broad, systemic influence on how society is ordered.

Idols in Our Culture

In his book *The Real American Dream: A Meditation on Hope,* Andrew Delbanco wrote, "I will use the word *culture* to mean the stories and symbols by which we try to hold back the melancholy suspicion that we live in a world without meaning."[99] At the heart of every culture is its main "Hope," what it tells its members that life is all about. Delbanco traces three phases of American civilization by looking at the fundamental hope of each era, which he names in sequence "God, Nation, and Self." In the first era "hope was chiefly expressed through a Christian story that gave meaning to suffering and pleasure alike and promised deliverance from death." In the second phase, "the Enlightenment removed a personal God . . . and substituted . . . the idea of a deified nation."[100] This second phase, which Delbanco says only began to pass away during the 1960s, transferred older ideas of sacredness to America itself, so that it came to see itself as the "Redeemer nation" whose system of government and way of life was the hope for the whole world.

Today the need for transcendence and meaning has detached itself from anything more important than the individual self and its freedom to be what it chooses. Among younger people, the older flag-waving "America first" mind-set is out. Now life is about creating a self through the maximization of individual freedom from the constraints of community.

Delbanco's cultural analysis is essentially an idol analysis. The age of "Self" explains why the maximization of profit has taken on the power that it has. Now we see the complexity of what shapes and drives us. Any dominant cultural "Hope" that is not God himself is a counterfeit god. Idols, then, do not only take individual form, but can be corporate and systemic. When we are completely immersed in a society of people who consider a particular idolatrous attachment normal, it becomes almost impossible to discern it for what it is.

We should not think that one culture is less idolatrous than the next. Traditional societies tend to make the family unit and the clan into an absolute, ultimate thing. This can lead to honor killings, the treatment of women as chattel, and violence toward gay people. Western, secular cultures make an idol out of individual freedom, and this leads to the breakdown of the family, rampant materialism, careerism, and the idolization of romantic love, physical beauty, and profit.

How can we be less enslaved by our cultural idols? Delbanco points out that in the beginning of our history society was built around God and religion. The answer to our cultural problem must be more religion, right? Not necessarily. Idolatry is so pervasive that it dominates this area as well.

Idols in Our Religion

An idol is something that we look to for things that only God can give. Idolatry functions widely inside religious communities when doctrinal truth is elevated to the position of a false god. This occurs when people rely on the rightness of their doctrine for their standing with God rather than on God himself and his grace. It is a subtle but deadly mistake. The sign that you have slipped into this form of self-justification is that you become what the book of Proverbs calls a "scoffer."[101] Scoffers always show contempt and disdain for opponents rather than graciousness. This is a sign that they do not see themselves as sinners saved by grace. Instead, their trust in the rightness of their views makes them feel superior.[102]

Another form of idolatry within religious communities turns spiritual gifts and ministry success into a counterfeit god. Spiritual gifts (talent, ability, performance, growth) are often mistaken for what the Bible calls spiritual "fruit" (love, joy, patience, humility, courage, gentleness).[103] Even ministers who believe with the mind that "I am only saved by grace" can come to feel in their heart that their standing with God depends largely on how many lives they are changing.

Another kind of religious idolatry has to do with moral living itself. As I have argued at length elsewhere,[104] the default mode of the human heart is to seek to control God and others through our moral performance. Because we have lived virtuous lives we feel that God (and the people we meet) owe us respect and support. Though we may give lip service to Jesus as our example and inspiration, we are still looking to ourselves and our own moral striving for salvation.

Delbanco explains how the great cultural shift known as the Enlightenment abandoned religious orthodoxy and put in God's place things like the American system or individual self-fulfillment. The results have not been good. Putting Nation in place of God leads to cultural imperialism, and putting Self in the place of God leads to many of the dysfunctional dynamics we have discussed throughout this book.[105] Why did our culture largely abandon God as its Hope? I believe it was because our religious communities have been and continue to be filled with these false gods. Making an idol out of doctrinal accuracy, ministry success, or moral rectitude leads to constant internal conflict, arrogance and self-righteousness, and oppression of those whose views differ. These toxic effects of religious idolatry have led to widespread disaffection with religion in general and Christianity in particular. Thinking we have tried God, we have turned to other Hopes, with devastating consequences.

The Mission of Jonah

We do not have only idols of the heart to confront. Corporate gods of the culture and religion can super-charge personal idols and create a poisonous mix. A poor young man who personally feels powerless can be easily swept up by social movements that fan racial and religious hatred. A young woman unloved by her family, and raised in a consumer culture of image and glamour, can become afflicted with an eating disorder. The idols that drive us are complex, many-layered, and largely hidden from us.

Perhaps the best example of this in the Bible is found in the famous story of Jonah. Most people think of it as a children's Sunday school lesson about a man swallowed by a big fish. On the contrary, it is a subtly crafted narrative about the idols that drive our actions on many levels and pull us farther from God even when we think we are doing his will. What is truly shocking about the story comes only at the very end, long after Jonah has left the fish far behind. The first, skillful sentence of the book introduces a plot full of dramatic tension.

The word of the LORD came to Jonah the son of Amittai, "Arise, go to Nineveh, that great city, and proclaim against her, for their evil has come up before my face."

Jonah 1:1–2[106]

From 2 Kings 14:25 we know that Jonah had called Israel's King Jeroboam to pursue an expansionist military policy to extend the nation's boundaries. His contemporaries, Amos and Hosea, were against the corruption of the royal administrations. Jonah, however, appears to have deliberately ignored the king's wrongdoing in his nationalistic zeal to build up his country's power and influence.[107] Such a prophet would have been stunned by God's command that he go to the city of Nineveh and preach to it.

Nineveh was the most powerful city in the world, the seat of the Assyrian Empire whose military threatened to overrun Israel and its neighbors. Doing anything that in any way benefited Assyria would have been seen as suicidal for Israel. Although the mission was only to "preach against" the city for its wickedness, there would have been no reason to send a warning unless there was a chance of judgment being averted, as Jonah knew full well (Jonah 4:1–2).

God was reaching out in mercy to the great enemy of his people—no more counterintuitive mission could have been imagined. God was sending a patriotic Jewish prophet to do this—no more unlikely emissary could have been chosen. God was asking him to do what he must have considered unconscionable. But that was the mission, and he was the missionary.

The Man on the Run

But Jonah arose to flee to Tarshish from the face of the LORD. He went down to Joppa and, finding a ship bound for Tarshish, he paid the fare and went down into it, to go with them to Tarshish, away from the face of the LORD.

Jonah 1:3

In deliberate contradiction of the charge to go east to Ninevah, Jonah arose and instead went to Tarshish, a town on the western rim of the known world. He did the very opposite of what God wanted him to do. Why? Jonah's internal motives are not fully revealed until chapter 4, but at this point, the text gives us several clues as to why he would so flagrantly disobey a direct divine command.

Jonah would have been afraid of failure. God was summoning a lone Hebrew prophet to walk into the most powerful city in the world and call it to get down on its knees before his God. The only possible outcome seemed to be mockery or death, with the second as likely as the first. Preachers want to go where they will be persuasive.

He would have been just as afraid, however, of the possibility of the mission's success, small as that might have been. Assyria was a cruel and violent empire. The empire was already demanding tribute from Israel, a kind of international protection money. Jonah was being called to warn Nineveh of God's wrath, to give them a chance to survive and continue to be a threat to Israel. As a patriotic Israelite, Jonah wanted no part of such a mission.

So why did he run? The answer is, again, idolatry, but of a very complex kind. Jonah had a personal idol. He wanted ministry success more than he wanted to obey God. Also, Jonah was shaped by a cultural idol. He put the national interests of Israel over obedience to God and the spiritual good of the Ninevites. Finally, Jonah had a religious idol, simple moral self-righteousness. He felt superior to the wicked, pagan Ninevites. He didn't want to see them saved. Jonah's cultural and personal idols had melded into a toxic compound that was completely hidden from him. It led him to rebel against the very God he was so proud of serving.

Jonah in the Deep

Jonah got on a boat in order to flee from God and his mission. But God sent a ferocious storm that threatened to sink the boat (Jonah 1:4–6). The sailors in the boat sensed that the storm was unusually violent, so they cast lots to see who had brought this calamity upon them. The lot fell on Jonah.

> *The men were seized by a great fear and—after he admitted that he was fleeing from the face of the Lord—they said to him: "How could you have done this!" Then they said to him, "What must we do to you, that the sea may become quiet for us, for the sea is more and more tempestuous?" He said to them, "Lift me up and hurl me into the sea; then the sea will become quiet for you, for I declare it is on my account that this great storm has come upon you."*

> Jonah 1:10–12

Afraid for their lives, the sailors did what Jonah asked. They threw him into the sea, and God provided a fish to save Jonah by swallowing him. The fish was God's provision for Jonah. It gave Jonah a chance to recover and repent. Inside the fish, Jonah offered a prayer to God.

Then Jonah prayed to the LORD his God from the belly of the fish, saying, "I call out to the LORD, out of my distress, and he answers me; I said, 'I am driven away from your sight; Nevertheless, I continue to gaze toward your holy temple.' . . . Those obeying empty idols forsake their own covenantal love. But I, with the voice of thanksgiving, will sacrifice to you; what I have vowed I will fulfill. Salvation comes only from the LORD!" And the LORD spoke to the fish, and it vomited Jonah out upon the dry land.

Jonah 1:17–2:1, 4, 8–10

He spoke of "those obeying empty idols. . . ." Idol worshippers were the people God had called Jonah to go to in Nineveh. But then he said something remarkable about them, that idolaters "forsake their own *chesedh.*" *Chesedh* is the Hebrew word for God's covenantal love, his redeeming, unconditional grace. This term had been used to describe God's relationship with Israel, his people. Now Jonah says that idol worshippers forsake "their *own* grace." It came to him like a thunderbolt that God's grace was as much theirs as it was his. Why? Because grace is grace. If it is truly grace, then no one was worthy of it at all, and that made all equal. And with that realization, he added, "Salvation comes only from the Lord!" It doesn't belong to any race or class of people, nor do religious people deserve it more than the irreligious. It does not come from any quality or merit in us at all. Salvation is only from the Lord.

There is an intriguing hint of self-insight in this prayer. What, according to Jonah, blocks the coming of grace into one's life? It is clinging to idols. Why, then, had Jonah himself so badly missed in his understanding of God's will and heart? The answer is—*his* idolatry. His fear of personal failure, his pride in his religion, and his fierce love of his country had coalesced into a deadly idolatrous compound that spiritually blinded him to the grace of God. As a result he did not want to extend that grace to an entire city that needed it. He wanted to see them all dead.

Race and Grace

Racial pride and cultural narrowness cannot coexist with the gospel of grace. They are mutually exclusive. One forces the other out. Because of the self-justifying nature of the human heart, it is natural to see our own culture or class characteristics as superior to everyone else's. But this natural tendency is arrested by the gospel.

We see this in Paul's confrontation with Peter in Galatians 2. Peter, as a Jewish apostle, had been raised to see Gentiles as spiritually "unclean," people with whom he should not eat. In ancient cultures, eating with someone symbolized openness and acceptance. When Paul saw Peter refusing to eat with Gentile Christians he confronted him about his racism. But how? Paul did not say, "You are breaking the rule against racism," but rather that Peter was "not acting in line with the gospel" (Galatians 2:14). Racial prejudice, Paul argued, was a denial of the very principle of grace salvation. He argued, "Peter, if we are all saved by grace alone—how can you feel superior to anyone? How can you continue to be racially and nationally exclusive? Use the gospel on your heart!" Peter, of course, did know the gospel at one level, but at a deeper level he wasn't fully shaped by it. He wasn't "walking in line" with it.

Those who are not secure in Christ cast about for spiritual life preservers with which to support their confidence, and in their frantic search they cling not only to the shreds of ability and righteousness they find in themselves, but they fix upon their race, their membership in a party, their familiar social and ecclesiastical patterns, and their culture as means of self-recommendation. The culture is put on as though it were armor against self-doubt, but it becomes a mental straitjacket which cleaves to the flesh and can never be removed except through comprehensive faith in the saving work of Christ.[108]

In the belly of the fish Jonah began to grasp what he had been missing, and why he had been so antagonistic to God's original call. Jonah had been called to go and preach grace to the greatest city in the world, but he hadn't understood that grace himself. Battered and humbled, he began to realize the truth. Salvation was by grace, and therefore it was available to anyone at all. His cultural idols seem to have been removed as all this dawned on him. And at that, the fish vomited him out. Jonah the prophet had another chance.

The Shocking Ending

Then the word of the LORD came to Jonah the second time, saying, "Arise, go to Nineveh, that great city, and proclaim to her the message that I tell you." So Jonah arose and set out for Nineveh, according to the word of the LORD. Now Nineveh was a very large city—three days' journey in breadth—and one important to God. Jonah went a day's journey into the city and then called out, "In forty days, Nineveh shall be overthrown!" And the people of Nineveh believed God. They called for a fast and put on sackcloth, from the greatest of them to the least. . . . When God examined their deeds, how they forsook their evil way, he renounced the disaster he had said he would do to them, and he did not carry it out. But what God did was so terrible in Jonah's eyes, that he burned with anger.

Jonah 3:1–5, 10; 4:1

Now comes the part of the story that is almost universally ignored. God again gave Jonah the call to go to Nineveh, and this time he obeyed. There he began to preach, and to Jonah's surprise and ours, the people of the city responded. They began to repent as some said, "Who knows? God may yet relent and with compassion turn from his fierce anger so we may not perish" (Verse 9). The result was that the city turned from "its evil ways," which Verse 8 describes as "their violence." The nation of Assyria was indeed exceedingly violent but here, at least temporarily, they showed remorse and willingness to reform.

God had mercy on them. There was no indication that the Ninevites became Jews or converted to full service of the God of Israel. Nothing like that happened, and yet God refrained from punishment, so predominant is his will to save rather than to punish.

Anyone reading this story would have expected the book to end on this wonderful note. Beyond hope, Jonah had returned from the dead and had fulfilled his mission, the Ninevites had repented and shown promise of turning from their violence and imperialism, and

God had shown how merciful and loving he is toward all peoples. All it would take now to complete the story would be a final verse, Jonah 3:11—"And Jonah returned to his own land rejoicing!"

But that is *not* what happened. The real shock of the story comes at the moment of what should have been Jonah's greatest triumph. He had preached to the most powerful city in the world and had brought it literally to its knees. Yet Nineveh's positive response to Jonah's preaching so infuriated him that he charged God with evil and asked God to kill him on the spot!

> *And he prayed to the LORD and said, "O LORD, is this not what I spoke of when I was still in my homeland? That is why I fled with haste to Tarshish; for I knew that you are a gracious and compassionate God, very patient, and abounding in steadfast love, and who also renounces plans for bringing disaster. Therefore now, O LORD, please take my life from me, for to me death is better than life."*

Jonah 4:1–3

The motives of Jonah's heart are finally revealed fully. "I knew it!" he says. "I knew you were a compassionate God, so quick to forgive, so eager to save, so unceasingly patient! I *knew* I couldn't trust you! That's the reason I ran away to begin with! I was afraid that if I got a God like you near these people and they made even a gesture in the direction of repentance you would forgive them. I've had it with you! I resign! Just take away my life!" There is no more astonishing speech in the Bible, or perhaps in all of ancient literature. Finally Jonah's idol was laid bare, revealing his abhorrence of this race and nation.

Jonah so loathed the Assyrian race that he saw God's forgiveness of them to be the worst thing that could have happened. He was willing to confront and denounce the Ninevites, but he could not love them. He didn't want them saved; he didn't want them to receive God's mercy.[109]

What happened? In the belly of the fish, Jonah had begun to grasp the idea that all human beings are equally unworthy of God's love and that therefore all human beings have equal access to God's grace. But Jonah's idolatries had reasserted themselves with a vengeance. His apprehension of God's grace in chapter 2 had been mainly intellectual. It had not penetrated his heart. Jonah stands as a warning that human hearts never change quickly or easily, even when a person is being mentored directly by God. Just as Paul had to confront Peter about how he had failed to use the gospel on his racism, so God's work with Jonah is incomplete.

Someone once said that if you want to know if there

are rats in your basement, you shouldn't walk down the steps slowly, making a lot of noise. Then you will look around and not see anything. If you want to know what is really down there, you have to surprise it by running and leaping down the steps quickly. Then you will see a bunch of little tails scurrying away. And so it is under stress, in real life experience, that the true nature of our hearts is revealed. For example, all Christians say and believe that Christ is their Savior, not their career or their wealth. What Christ thinks of us is what matters, not human approval. That is what we *say*. But while Jesus is our Savior in principle, other things still maintain functional title to our hearts. Jonah shows us that it is one thing to believe the gospel with our minds, and another to work it deep into our hearts so it affects everything we think, feel, and do. He is still being largely controlled by idolatry.

Idols, Thinking, and Feeling

Idolatry has distorted Jonah's thinking. [110] He goes on a tirade that most people would think insane. How could Jonah be furious that God is a God of compassion, love, and patience?! For the same reason that lovesick Jacob could be so easily duped and greedy Zacchaeus could betray his country and everyone around him. They were all blinded by their idols.

When an idol gets a grip on your heart, it spins out a whole set of false definitions of success and failure and happiness and sadness. It redefines reality in terms of itself. Nearly everyone thinks that an all-powerful God of love, patience, and compassion is a good thing. But if, because of your idol, your ultimate good is the power and status of your people, then anything that gets in the way of it is, by definition, bad. When God's love prevented him from smashing Israel's enemy, Jonah, because of his idol, was forced to see God's love as a bad thing. In the end idols can make it possible to call evil good and good evil.[111]

Idols distort not only our thinking, but also our feelings.

And the LORD said, "Is it good for you to burn with such anger?" Jonah then left the city and sat down just east of it and made a shelter for himself there. He sat under it in the shade, waiting to see what would happen to the city. To deliver him from his dejection, the LORD God appointed a qiqayon plant that grew rapidly up over Jonah, to be a shade over his head. And Jonah was delighted and glad for the plant. But at the break of dawn the next day, God appointed a worm that attacked the qiqayon plant, so that it withered. And when the sun rose higher, God appointed a cutting east wind, and the

*sun beat down on the head of Jonah so that he was
faint and weak. And he longed to die, thinking, "It
is better for me to die than to live." But God said to
Jonah, "Is it good for you to be so angry and dejected
over the plant?" And he said, "Yes, it is. I am angry
and dejected enough to die."*

Jonah 4:4–9

Jonah left the city he despised and made himself a
shelter from the sun. He was still hoping that God might
relent from his relenting and smite Nineveh. But God's
concern was now with Jonah. He allowed a "*gigayon*
plant," a fast-growing vine, to grow up and make his
shelter cool and shady. The greenery and the comfort
were a consolation for the despondent prophet. But
then God brought a new, though small-scale, disappointment into his life, by having the plant die. Jonah's
emotions were so raw that this new discouragement
pushed him back to the edge. Again he was too angry
to live. This time, when God asked him whether his
anger was warranted, Jonah retorted that it was, that
he was "angry enough to die."

God confronted him about this. God did not say
that anger is wrong, since he himself regularly speaks
about his own "fierce anger" against injustice and
evil. However, Jonah's anger was unwarranted and
disproportionate.

Idolatry distorts our feelings. Just as idols are good things turned into ultimate things, so the desires they generate become paralyzing and overwhelming. Idols generate false beliefs such as "if I cannot achieve X, then my life won't be valid" or "since I have lost or failed Y, now I can never be happy or forgiven again." These beliefs magnify ordinary disappointments and failures into life-shattering experiences.

A young woman named Mary was an accomplished musician who once attended my church. For many years she had battled mental illness and had checked in and out of psychiatric institutions. She gave me permission as her pastor to speak to her therapist so my pastoral guidance to her could be well-informed. "Mary virtually worships her parents' approval of her," her counselor told me, "and they always wanted her to be a world-class artist. She is quite good, but she's never reached the top of her profession, and she cannot live with the idea that she has disappointed her parents." Medications helped to manage her depression, but they could not get to the root of it. Her problem was a false belief, driven by an idol. She told herself, "If I cannot be a well-known violinist, I have let down my parents and my life is a failure." She was distressed and guilty enough to die. When Mary began to believe the gospel, that she was saved by grace, not by musicianship, and that, "though my father and mother forsake me, the Lord shall take me in" (Psalm 27:10), she began to get relief from her idolatrous need for her parents' approval. In time her depression and anxiety began to lift, and she was able to reenter her life and musical career.

There is legitimate guilt that is removed through repentance and restitution, and then there is irremediable guilt. When people say, "I know God forgives me, but I can't forgive myself," they mean that they have failed an idol, whose approval is more important to them than God's. Idols function like gods in our lives, and so if we make career or parental approval our god and we fail it, then the idol curses us in our hearts for the rest of our lives. We can't shake the sense of failure.

When idolatry is mapped onto the future—when our idols are threatened—it leads to paralyzing fear and anxiety. When it is mapped onto the past—when we fail our idols—it leads to irremediable guilt. When idolatry is mapped onto the present life—when our idols are blocked or removed by circumstances—it roils us with anger and despair.[112]

All that was happening in Jonah's heart. Why had Jonah lost the will to live? You don't lose your desire to live unless you have lost your meaning in life. His meaning in life was the freedom of his nation. That is a good thing to want, but it had become a supreme thing. Therefore, the Assyrians filled him with deep hate and anger because they were an obstacle to obtaining the idol. Now it was God and his mercy that filled Jonah with anger and despair, because the Lord was an omnipotent roadblock to the future for Israel that Jonah wanted.

The True Jonah

And the LORD said, "You grieved over the gigayon plant, which you did not plant, you did not make grow, and which came into being and perished in one night. And should I not have compassion for Nineveh, that great city, in which there are more than 120,000 persons who do not know their right hand from their left, and so much livestock?"

Jonah 4:10–11

God confronted Jonah with the fact that he was more upset about his sunburn than he was about thousands of people who "did not know their right hand from their left." His idolatrous love for his own country and his moral self-righteousness had removed Jonah's compassion for the great cities and nations of the world. All he cared about was his own country.

God was different. He ended his instruction to Jonah by drawing a deliberate contrast between Jonah and himself. He had asked Jonah to leave his comfort zone and his safety, and to go in love to minister to a people who might harm him. At first, Jonah didn't go at all, and then he went, but without compassion. God responded: "You did not have compassion on this city, but I will." God implied that he would love the wicked, violent city in a way Jonah had refused to do.

What did that mean? How did God do what Jonah did not?

Centuries later, someone came who said to his astonished listeners that he was the ultimate Jonah (Matthew 12:39–41). When Jesus Christ came to earth, he was leaving the ultimate comfort zone, in order to come and minister not just to a people who *might* harm him, but to people who would. And to save them, he would have to do much more than preach, he would have to die for them. While the original Jonah was merely thought to be dead, Jesus actually died and rose again. It was what Jesus called the sign of Jonah (Matthew 12:31).

Consider another way in which Jesus was the ultimate Jonah. In Mark 4 we have an account from Jesus's life that deliberately evoked the Old Testament story. There was a terrible storm and, like Jonah, Jesus was asleep in the midst of it. Like the sailors, Jesus's disciples were terrified and woke him up to say that they were going to perish. In both cases the storm was miraculously calmed and those in the boat were saved by the power of God.

But here is the great difference. Jonah was thrown only into a storm of wind and water. Jesus on the Cross, however, was thrown into the ultimate storm—of all the divine justice and punishment that we deserve for our wrongdoing. When I struggle with my idols, I think of Jesus, voluntarily bowing his head into that ultimate storm, taking it on frontally, for me. He sank in that storm of terror so I would not fear any other storm in my life. If he did that for me, then I know my value, confidence, and mission in life all rest in him. Storms here on earth can take away many things, even my physical life, but not my Life.

God hinted to Jonah that he would love the great, lost cities of the earth in a way that Jonah would not. In the gospel of Jesus Christ, the true Jonah, that commitment was fulfilled.

Jonah and Us

The book of Jonah ends with a question. God asks Jonah: "Shouldn't your love be like mine? Will you come out of your self-absorption and idolatry and begin to live for me and for others?" We wait for an answer, and it never comes! Because the book ends.

The ending is brilliant and satisfying. It's satisfying because we don't need to wonder whether Jonah repented and saw the light. He must have. How do we know? Well, how else would we know this story, unless Jonah told it to someone? And who would *ever* tell a story in which he is seen as an evil fool on every page, except a man in whom God's grace had reached the center of his heart?

Why, though, are we not shown Jonah's response in the book? It is as if God aimed an arrow of loving rebuke at Jonah's heart, set it a-fly, and suddenly Jonah vanishes, leaving us in its path. The question is coming right at us, because you are Jonah and I am Jonah. We are so enslaved to our idols that we don't care about people who are Different, who live in the big cities, or who are just in our own families but very hard to love. Are we, like Jonah, willing to change? If we are, then we must look to the Ultimate Jonah, and to his sign, the death and resurrection of Jesus Christ.

SEVEN

❧⦿⦿❧

THE END OF COUNTERFEIT GODS

Nothing Is More Common

The seventeenth-century English minister David Clarkson preached one of the most comprehensive and searching sermons on counterfeit gods ever written.[113] About idolatry he said, "Though few will own it, nothing is more common." If we think of our soul as a house, he said, "idols are set up in every room, in every faculty." We prefer our own wisdom to God's wisdom, our own desires to God's will, and our own reputation to God's honor. Clarkson looked at human relationships and showed how we have a tendency to make them more influential and important to us than God. In fact, he showed that "many make even their enemies their god . . . when they are more troubled, disquieted, and perplexed at apprehensions of danger to their liberty, estates, and lives from men" than they are concerned about God's displeasure.[114] The human heart is indeed a factory that mass-produces idols.

Is there any hope? Yes, if we begin to realize that idols cannot simply be removed. They must be replaced. If you only try to uproot them, they grow back; but they can be supplanted. By what? By God himself, of course. But by *God* we do not mean a general belief in his existence. Most people have that, yet their souls are riddled with idols. What we need is a living encounter with God.

Jacob, whom we met in Chapter Two, certainly believed in God, but he needed something more to defeat the counterfeit gods that enslaved him. In Genesis 32 he found it. This is one of the most powerful and dramatic narratives in the Bible. It is also one of the most mysterious, but it clearly stands as the centerpiece of Jacob's life.

The Returning Brother

Jacob had fled to a far country and despite many struggles had prospered there. Yet his uncle Laban and his cousins were resentful and jealous of Jacob (Genesis 31:1–2). He realized that he had to leave or face strife, perhaps even violent conflict. At last he decided to return to his homeland with his large family, his two wives, Leah and Rachel, and all their servants, flocks, and herds.

The author of Genesis recounted a short but significant subplot about Jacob's wife Rachel, who, as she left, stole her father Laban's household idols (Genesis 31:19). Why did she do it? It may have been a kind of spiritual insurance policy. Maybe, thought Rachel, the Lord would help her the next time she was in trouble, as he seemed to help Leah, but if not, she would call on the old gods. However, the Lord cannot be added to a life as one more hedge against failure. He is not one more resource to use to help us achieve our agenda. He *is* a whole new agenda. Rachel had not learned this. The family that was to bring the salvation of the Lord into the future was deeply flawed and in need of grace.

Jacob set out for his homeland with his entire family and estate. As he drew near he received some alarming news. "We went to your brother Esau, and now he is coming to meet you and four hundred men are with him." (Genesis 32:6) Jacob's worst fears seemed to be realized. Why else would Esau be coming with a small army except to attack him? He sprang into action. First he prayed to God for help. Then he sent an enormous gift of livestock to Esau with some servants. After that he divided his family and company in half, thinking that if Esau attacked one half of his people the other half would have time to escape (Genesis 32:7–8). After all the preparations had been made, and both halves of his company had been sent on ahead, Jacob sat down to spend the night alone.

The Struggle for Blessing

In Jacob's mind, the next day would be the climax of his life. All his life he had been wrestling with Esau. In their mother's womb, the twins Esau and Jacob had been unusually active, "striving with each other" (Genesis 25:22). As they grew up, Jacob contended with Esau for the favor and love of their father and for the honor and leadership of their family. Their father constantly favored Esau over Jacob, and there are few things more wounding to a son. Finally the day came that Isaac was to give Esau the ritual blessing that went with his birthright, the lion's share of the family estate. Jacob, however, disguised himself as Esau and fooled his nearly blind father just long enough to get him to pronounce the blessing. Then he ran. When Esau discovered what had happened he vowed to kill Jacob. So Jacob had fled for his life into exile.

Why did Jacob steal Esau's blessing? Modern readers find his motives difficult to understand. Surely Jacob knew his ruse would be discovered quickly, and that Isaac would never have actually given Jacob the majority of the family's wealth. All Jacob got was the ceremonial affirmation. Why did he lose so much to gain so little? I believe it was because Jacob, even under false pretenses, longed to hear his father say, "I delight in you more than anyone else in the world!" Every human being, then, needs blessing. We all need assurance of our unique value from some outside source. The love and admiration of those you most love and admire is above all rewards. We are all looking for this deep admiration, looking for it from our parents, our spouse, and our peers.

Jacob's life had been one long wrestling match to get blessing. He had wrestled with Esau to hear it from his father's lips. He had wrestled with Laban to find it in Rachel's face. But it hadn't worked. He was still needy and empty inside. The relationships within his own family were stormy. His idolatry of Rachel and her children had poisoned the lives of Leah and her children, and it would bear bitter fruit in the future.

And now Esau was on his way, the man who had kept him from his father's love, from his inheritance, from his destiny, from happiness. He was coming with an army. Tomorrow would be the last battle. It was not surprising that Jacob wanted to spend this last night alone to prepare for the day of reckoning. But that night, in the deep darkness, he was unexpectedly attacked by a lone figure, and they wrestled for hours.

The Mysterious Stranger

The dramatic story is depicted with great economy.

So Jacob was left alone, and a man wrestled with him till daybreak. When the man saw that he could not overpower him, he touched the socket of Jacob's hip so that his hip was wrenched as he wrestled with the man. Then the man said, "Let me go, for it is daybreak." But Jacob replied, "I will not let you go unless you bless me." The man asked him, "What is your name?" "Jacob," he answered. Then the man said, "Your name will no longer be Jacob, but Israel, because you have struggled with God and with men and have overcome." Jacob said, "Please tell me your name." But he replied, "Why do you ask my name?" Then he blessed him there. So Jacob called the place Peniel, saying, "It is because I saw God face to face, and yet my life was spared." The sun rose above him as he passed Peniel, and he was limping because of his hip.

Genesis 32:24–31

Who was this mysterious figure? The narrator deliberately obscures his identity to the reader, but leaves a few clues. First, there was the powerful "touch" (Verse 28). The Hebrew word translated "touch" literally meant the lightest contact or tap. The wrestler merely touched Jacob's hip with his finger and it was instantly ripped out of its socket, permanently disabling him. It was now clear that the wrestler had been holding back so as not to kill Jacob. He had enormous, superhuman power.

Also, the figure insisted he must leave as dawn neared. Why? Jacob knew that no one could look upon God's face and live (Exodus 33:20). Afterward, Jacob realized that this was the reason the wrestler had wanted to leave before the sun came up. It was for Jacob's own protection, for, as Jacob said, he "saw God's face and lived." This may mean that in the first grayness of in-cipient dawn he was able to make out the lines on the face of the divine wrestler just before he vanished. Had he seen God's face in the clear light of day, he would have perished.

Winning through Weakness

Jacob recognized who he was wrestling with—God himself! When he realized this, and saw the sun com-ing up, Jacob did the most astonishing thing he had ever done. He did not do the rational thing, which would have been to cry out, "Let me go! Let me go! I don't want to die!" Instead he did the very opposite. He held on tight, and said, "I will not let you go until you bless me!"

Jacob was saying something like this.

What an idiot I've been! Here is what I've been looking for all my life. The blessing of God! I looked for it in the approval of my father. I looked for it in the beauty of Rachel. But it was in you. Now I won't let you go until you bless me. Nothing else matters. I don't care if I die in the process, because if I don't have God's blessing, I've got nothing. Nothing else will do.

As a result, we read, God "blessed him there." Wonderful, mysterious words. A blessing in the Bible is always verbal, so God must have spoken words into Jacob's heart. What were they? We are not told. Was it anything like the voice of blessing that was spoken from heaven over the great descendent of Jacob—"You are my son, whom I love, with you I am well pleased"? (Mark 1:11) We don't know the exact words, but there is nothing greater than the blessing of God. And Jacob walked away as the very picture of one who has believed the gospel, for he had been permanently lamed, yet permanently fulfilled. He had been humbled, yet emboldened—all at the same time.

So Jacob won! God said, "You have struggled with God . . . and overcome." He was victorious because, once he realized the divinity of this mysterious wrestler, he did not flee but rather held on. Jacob finally got the blessing that he had longed for all his life. Soon afterward, Jacob met Esau and his band of men, and to his relief he learned that Esau was coming to greet him in peace and welcome him home. So that feud was ended.

The Weakness of God

The reader of the life of Jacob might be perplexed at this point. In no episode throughout the life of Jacob does he ever emerge as the hero. He never behaved as a moral paragon; instead he continually acted in foolish, devious, or even vicious ways. He didn't seem to deserve any blessing from God at all. Why, if God is holy and just, was he so gracious to Jacob? Why would God feign weakness to keep from killing him, then give him clues as to who he was, then bless him for no better reason than that he held on desperately?

The answer to our question comes later in the Bible, when the Lord again appeared as a man. In the darkness with Jacob, God feigned weakness in order to save Jacob's life. But in the darkness of Calvary, the Lord appeared as a man and became truly weak to save us. Jacob held on in obedience at the risk of his life, in order to gain blessing for himself. But when facing the Cross, though he could have turned aside, Jesus held on in obedience at the cost of his life, in order to gain the blessing, not for himself, but for us.

> *Christ redeemed us from the curse of the law by becoming a curse for us. . . . He redeemed us in order that the blessing given to Abraham might come to the Gentiles through Christ Jesus, so that by faith we might receive the promise of the Spirit.*
>
> Galatians 3:13–14

Why could Jacob come so close to God and still live? It was because Jesus came in weakness and died on the Cross to pay the penalty for our sin. The blessing of God, promised to Abraham, "comes . . . through Christ Jesus, so that by faith we might receive the promise of the Spirit." What was that "promise of the Spirit"? Later in Galatians, Paul writes that "God sent the Spirit of his Son into our hearts who cries out, 'Abba, Father'"(Galatians 4:6). *Abba* was the Aramaic diminutive word for "father," roughly to be translated "papa." It is a term of trusting confidence that a little child has in a parent's love. Paul is saying that, if you believe the gospel, the Spirit will make God's love and blessing an existential reality in your heart.

Have you heard God's blessing in your inmost being? Are the words *"You are my beloved child, in whom I delight"* an endless source of joy and strength?

Have you sensed, through the Holy Spirit, God speaking them to you? That blessing—the blessing through the Spirit that is ours through Christ—is what Jacob received, and it is the only remedy against idolatry. Only that blessing makes idols unnecessary. As with Jacob, we usually discover this only after a life of "looking for blessing in all the wrong places." It often takes an experience of crippling weakness for us to finally discover it. That is why so many of the most God-blessed people limp as they dance for joy.

For the foolishness of God is wiser than man's wisdom, and the weakness of God is stronger than man's strength.

1 Corinthians 1:25

Epilogue:
FINDING AND REPLACING YOUR IDOLS

The Importance of Discerning Idols

It is impossible to understand your heart or your culture if you do not discern the counterfeit gods that influence them. In Romans 1:21–25 Saint Paul shows that idolatry is not only one sin among many, but what is fundamentally wrong with the human heart:

> *For although they knew God, they neither glorified him as God nor gave thanks to him. . . . They exchanged the truth of God for a lie, and worshipped and served created things rather than the Creator.*
>
> Romans 1:21, 25

Paul goes on to make a long list of sins that create misery and evil in the world, but they all find their roots in this soil, the inexorable human drive for "god-making." [115] In other words, *idolatry is always the reason we ever do anything wrong.* No one grasped this better than Martin Luther. In his *Large Catechism* (1529) and in his *Treatise on Good Works* he wrote that the Ten Commandments begin with a commandment against idolatry. Why does this come first? Because, he argued, the fundamental motivation behind lawbreaking is idolatry. [116] We never break the other commandments without breaking the first one. Why do we fail to love or keep promises or live unselfishly? Of course, the general answer is "because we are weak and sinful," but the specific answer in any actual circumstance is that there is something you feel you *must* have to be happy, something that is more important to your heart than God himself. We would not lie unless we first had made something—human approval, reputation, power over others, financial advantage—more important and valuable to our hearts than the grace and favor of God. The secret to change is to identify and dismantle the counterfeit gods of your heart. [117]

It is impossible to understand a culture without discerning its idols. The Jewish philosophers Halbertal and Margalit make it clear that idolatry is not simply a form of ritual worship, but a whole sensibility and pattern of life based on finite values and making created things into godlike absolutes. In the Bible, therefore, turning from idols always includes a rejection of the culture that the idols produce. God tells Israel that they must not only reject the other nations' gods, but "you shall not follow their practices" (Exodus 23:24). There is no way to challenge idols without doing cultural criticism, and there is no way to do cultural criticism without discerning and challenging idols.[118] A good example of this is the preaching of Saint Paul in Athens (Acts 17) and Ephesus (Acts 19). Paul challenged the gods of the city of Ephesus (Acts 19:26), which led to such an alteration in the spending patterns of new converts that it changed the local economy. That in turn touched off a riot led by local merchants. Contemporary observers have often noted that modern Christians are just as materialistic as everyone else in our culture. Could this be because our preaching of the gospel does not, like Saint Paul's, include the exposure of our culture's counterfeit gods?

Identifying Idols

I am not asking whether or not you have rival gods. I assume that we all do; they are hidden in every one of us.[119] The question is: What do we do about them? How can we become increasingly clear-sighted rather than remaining in their power? How can we be freed from our idols so we can make sound decisions and wise choices that are best for us and those around us? How can we discern our idols?

One way requires that we look at our imagination. Archbishop William Temple once said, "Your religion is what you do with your solitude."[120] In other words, the true god of your heart is what your thoughts effortlessly go to when there is nothing else demanding your attention. What do you enjoy daydreaming about? What occupies your mind when you have nothing else to think about? Do you develop potential scenarios about career advancement? Or material goods such as a dream home? Or a relationship with a particular person? One or two daydreams are no an indication of idolatry. Ask rather, what do you habitually think about to get joy and comfort in the privacy of your heart?

Another way to discern your heart's true love is to look at how you spend your money. Jesus said, "Where your treasure is, there is your heart also" (Matthew 6:21). Your money flows most effortlessly toward your heart's greatest love. In fact, the mark of an idol is that you spend too much money on it, and you must try to exercise self-control constantly. As Saint Paul has written, if God and his grace is the thing in the world you love most, you will give your money away to ministry, charity, and the poor in astonishing amounts (2 Corinthians 8:7–9). Most of us, however, tend to overspend on clothing, or on our children, or on status symbols such as homes and cars. Our patterns of spending reveal our idols.

A third way to discern idols works best for those who have professed a faith in God. You may regularly go to a place of worship. You may have a full, devout set of doctrinal beliefs. You may be trying very hard to believe and obey God. However, what is your real, daily functional salvation? What are you really living for, what is your real—not your professed—god? A good way to discern this is how you respond to unanswered prayers and frustrated hopes. If you ask for something that you don't get, you may become sad and disappointed. Then you go on. Hey, life's not over. Those are not your functional masters. But when you pray and work for something and you don't get it and you respond with explosive anger or deep despair, then you may have found your real god. Like Jonah, you become angry enough to die.

A final test works for everyone. Look at your most uncontrollable emotions.[121] Just as a fisherman looking for fish knows to go where the water is roiling, look for your idols at the bottom of your most painful emotions, especially those that never seem to lift and that drive you to do things you know are wrong. If you are angry, ask, "Is there something here too important to me, something I must have at all costs?" Do the same thing with strong fear or despair and guilt. Ask yourself, "Am I so scared, because something in my life is being threatened that I think is a necessity when it is not?

Am I so down on myself because I have lost or failed at something that I think is a necessity when it is not?" If you are overworking, driving yourself into the ground with frantic activity, ask yourself, "Do I feel that I *must* have this thing to be fulfilled and significant?" When you ask questions like that, when you "pull your emotions up by the roots," as it were, you will often find your idols clinging to them.

David Powlison writes:

> . . . that most basic question which God poses to each human heart: "Has something or someone besides Jesus the Christ taken title to your heart's functional trust, preoccupation, loyalty, service, fear and delight? Questions . . . bring some of people's idol systems to the surface. 'To who or what do you look for life-sustaining stability, security and acceptance? . . . What do you really want and expect [out of life]? What would [really] make you happy? What would make you an acceptable person? Where do you look for power and success?' These questions or similar ones tease out whether we serve God or idols, whether we look for salvation from Christ or from false saviors."[122]

Replacing Idols

In Paul's letter to the Colossians he exhorted them to "put to death" the evil desires of the heart, including "greed, which is idolatry" (Colossians 3:5). But how? Paul laid out the way in the preceding verses.

Since, then, you have been raised with Christ, set your hearts on things above, where Christ is seated at the right hand of God. Set your minds on things above, not on earthly things. For you died, and your life is now hidden with Christ in God. When Christ, who is your life, appears, then you also will appear with him in glory. Put to death, therefore, whatever belongs to your earthly nature: sexual immorality, impurity, lust, evil desires and greed, which is idolatry.

Colossians 3:1–5

Idolatry is not just a failure to obey God, it is a setting of the whole heart on something besides God. This cannot be remedied only by repenting that you have an idol, or using willpower to try to live differently. Turning from idols is not less than those two things, but it is also far more. "Setting the mind and heart on things above" where "your life is hid with Christ in God" (Colossians 3:1–3) means appreciation, rejoicing, and resting in what Jesus has done for you. It entails joyful worship, a sense of God's reality in prayer. Jesus must become more beautiful to your imagination, more attractive to your heart, than your idol. That is what will replace your counterfeit gods. If you uproot the idol and fail to "plant" the love of Christ in its place, the idol will grow back.

Rejoicing and repentance must go together. Repentance without rejoicing will lead to despair. Rejoicing without repentance is shallow and will only provide passing inspiration instead of deep change. Indeed, it is when we rejoice over Jesus's sacrificial love for us most fully that, paradoxically, we are most truly convicted of our sin. When we repent out of fear of consequences, we are not really sorry for the sin, but for ourselves. Fear-based repentance ("I'd better change or God will get me") is really self-pity. In fear-based repentance, we don't learn to hate the sin for itself, and it doesn't lose its attractive power. We learn only to refrain from it for our own sake. But when we rejoice over God's sacrificial, suffering love for us—seeing what it cost him to save us from sin—we learn to hate the sin for what it is. We see what the sin cost God. What most assures us of God's unconditional love (Jesus's costly death) is what that most convicts us of the evil of sin. Fear-based repentance makes us hate ourselves. Joy-based repentance makes us hate the sin.

Rejoicing in Christ is also crucial because idols are almost always *good* things. If we have made idols out of work and family, we do not want to stop loving our work and our family. Rather, we want to love Christ so much *more* that we are not enslaved by our attachments. "Rejoicing" in the Bible is much deeper than simply being happy about something. Paul directed that we should "rejoice in the Lord always" (Philippians 4:4), but this cannot mean "always feel happy," since no one can command someone to always have a particular emotion. To rejoice is to treasure a thing, to assess its value to you, to reflect on its beauty and importance until your heart rests in it and tastes the sweetness of it. "Rejoicing" is a way of praising God until the heart is sweetened and rested, and until it relaxes its grip on anything else it thinks that it needs.

Putting the Gospel on Video

Henry and Kevin had both lost their jobs because of an unfair action by their bosses, and they came to see me for counseling within a year of each other. Henry forgave his boss and moved on and was doing very well, while Kevin could not move past it; he stayed bitter and cynical, and it affected his future career path. Some people tried to help him by working on his emotions. The more sympathy people showed Kevin, the more he felt justified in his anger and the more his self-pity grew. Other people tried to work directly on his will ("get past it and move on"). That did not work either. The gospel works in a different way. It does not work directly on the emotions or the will. The gospel asks, *What is operating in the place of Jesus Christ as your real, functional salvation and Savior?* What are you looking to in order to justify yourself? Whatever it is, is a counterfeit god, and to make a change in your life, you must identify it and reject it as such.

Kevin was looking to his career to prove himself, and when something went wrong, he felt condemned. He was paralyzed because the very foundations of his identity were falling apart. He made no progress until he saw that he had made his career his self-salvation. It was not just that he had to forgive his boss; his real problem was that something besides Jesus Christ was functioning as his Savior. There is always something underneath your inordinate and out-of-control problems, desires, patterns, attitudes, and emotions. Until you find out what it is you cannot have life and peace.

Kevin came to see that though he technically believed he was loved with God's costly grace, it wasn't an absorbing truth that had captured his heart and imagination. What his boss said to him was more real and affecting to his heart than what the King of the universe had said. It is possible to listen to an audio recording while doing other things around the house, but to watch and listen to a visual presentation is much more absorbing. It fills your vision. In the same way, you may know about the love of Christ with your head but not with your heart, as in Kevin's case. How can that be remedied? How can we put the gospel truths "on video" in our lives so that they shape all we feel and do?

This takes what are called "the spiritual disciplines," such as private prayer, corporate worship, and meditation.[123] The disciplines take cognitive knowledge and make it a life-shaping reality in our hearts and imaginations. Spiritual disciplines are basically forms of *worship,* and it is worship that is the final way to replace the idols of your heart. You cannot get relief simply by figuring out your idols intellectually. You have to actually get the peace that Jesus gives, and that only comes as you worship. Analysis can help you discover truths, but then you need to "pray them in" to your heart. That takes time. It is a process about which there is much to say, but we cannot take it up in this book.

Be Patient

I believe that this process will take our entire lives. In the 1960s and '70s Interstate 79 was being built in western Pennsylvania. My wife, Kathy, often drove this route from her home in Pittsburgh to her college in Meadville, Pennsylvania, and to the family vacation spot on Lake Erie. For years the highway remained uncompleted at one spot, where there was a particularly nasty swamp. On at least one occasion, construction workers parked a bulldozer overnight on what seemed to be solid ground. However, by morning they discovered that it had sunk. Often when they put down pilings in the attempt to find bedrock, the pilings disappeared.

Our hearts are like that. We think we've learned about grace, set our idols aside, and reached a place where we're serving God not for what we're going to get from him but for who he is. There's a certain sense in which we spend our entire lives thinking we've reached the bottom of our hearts and finding it is a false bottom. Mature Christians are not people who have completely hit the bedrock. I do not believe that is possible in this life. Rather, they are people who know how to keep drilling and are getting closer and closer.

The great pastor and hymn-writer John Newton once wrote about this struggle:

If I may speak my own experience, I find that to keep my eye simply on Christ, as my peace and my life, is by far the hardest part of my calling. . . . It seems easier to deny self in a thousand instances of outward conduct, than in its ceaseless endeavors to act as a principle of righteousness and power.[124]

The man or woman who knows the difference that Newton refers to—the difference between obeying rules of outward conduct rather than setting your heart on Christ as your peace and your life—is on the road to freedom from the counterfeit gods that control us.

NOTES

INTRODUCTION—The Idol Factory

1. All of these suicides occurred between May 2008 and April 2009. They were compiled on a blog post at http://copy cateffect.blogspot.com/2009/04/recess-x.html

2. Alexis de Tocqueville, *Democracy in America*, trans. George Lawrence (New York, Harper, 1988), p. 296, quoted in Andrew Delbanco, *The Real American Dream: A Meditation on Hope* (Cambridge, Mass.: Harvard University Press, 1999), p. 3.

3. *Ibid.*

4. David Brooks, "The Rank-Link Imbalance," *New York Times,* March 14, 2008.

5. The use of idolatry as a major category for psychological and sociocultural analysis has been gaining steam again in the last fifteen years in the academic world. First there was the heyday of Feuerbach, Marx, and Nietzsche, who used the vocabulary of "idolatry" to critique religion and Christianity

Notes

itself, saying the church had created God in its own image, to further its own interests. See Merold Westphal, *Suspicion and Faith: The Religious Uses of Modern Atheism* (The Bronx: Fordham, 1999). After neglect, the concept has been given groundbreaking, serious academic treatment by two prominent Jewish philosophers, Moshe Halbertal and Avishai Margalit, in *Idolatry* (Cambridge, Mass.: Harvard University Press, 1992). Building on this work, there has been a recent wave of serious scholarship on the subject. For example, see Stephen C. Barton, ed., *Idolatry: False Worship in the Bible, Early Judaism, and Christianity* (London and New York: T and T Clark, 2007), G. K. Beale, *We Become What We Worship: A Biblical Theology of Idolatry* (Downers Grove, Ill.: InterVarsity Press, 2008), Edward P. Meadors, *Idolatry and the Hardening of the Heart: A Study in Biblical Theology* (London and New York: T and T Clark, 2006), Brian S. Rosner, *Greed as Idolatry: The Origin and Meaning of a Pauline Metaphor* (Grand Rapids, Mich.: Eerdmans, 2007).

6. In the Bible, idolatry includes, of course, the ritual worship of gods other than the true God of Israel. It means to bow down or to "kiss the hand" or make sacrifices to the gods of other religions and nations (Exodus 20:3; 23:13; Job 31:26–28; Psalms 44:20–21). Anyone who does so forfeits God's salvation (Jonah 2:8). But the Bible makes it clear that we cannot confine idolatry to literal bowing down before the images of false gods. It can be done internally in the soul and heart without being done externally and literally (Ezekiel 14:3ff). It is substituting some cre-

ated thing for God in the heart, in the center of the life. For example, the prophet Habakkuk speaks of the Babylonians, "whose own strength is their god" (Habakkuk 1:11) and of their military power, to which they "sacrifice . . . and burn incense" (Habakkuk 1:16). In Ezekiel 16 and Jeremiah 2–3, the prophets charge Israel with idolatry because they entered into protective treaties with Egypt and Assyria. These treaties offered the payment of high taxes and political subjugation in exchange for military protection. The prophets considered this idolatry because Israel was relying on Egypt and Assyria to give them the security that only God could give them (Halbertal and Margalit, *Idolatry*. pp. 5–6). When King Saul disobeyed the word of the Lord from Samuel and began to conduct business and foreign policy in a way typical of imperialistic powers, the prophet Samuel told him that arrogant disobedience to the Lord *was* idolatry (I Sam 15:23). In the Bible, then, idolatry is looking to your own wisdom and competence, or to some other created thing, to provide the power, approval, comfort, and security that only God can provide. One of the classic Protestant expositions of idolatry is found in the Puritan David Clarkson's sermon "Soul Idolatry Excludes Men Out of Heaven" (*The Works of David Clarkson* [Edinburgh: James Nichols, 1864], vol. 2). Clarkson distinguishes between "External" idolatry, which consists in literal bowing down to a physical image, and "Internal" idolatry, which consists of an act of the soul. "When the mind is most taken up with an object and the heart and affections most set upon it, this is *soul* worship; and this is . . . the honor due only to the Lord, to have the first, the highest place, both in our minds and hearts and endeavors" (p. 300).

7. Tom Shippey, *J. R. R. Tolkien: Author of the Century* (New York: Houghton Mifflin, 2000), p. 36.

8. Near the end of the magisterial book *Idolatry* by Moshe Halbertal and Avishai Margalit, they summarize the nature of idolatry this way. "Granting something ultimate value does not necessarily mean attributing a set of metaphysical divine attributes; the act of granting ultimate value involves a life of full devotion and ultimate commitment to something or someone. Absolute value can be conferred upon many things. . . . In this *extension* of worship, religious attitude is perceived not as part of metaphysics or as an expression of customary rituals, but as a form of absolute devotion, an attitude that makes something into a godlike being. What makes something into an absolute is that it is both overriding and demanding. It claims to stand superior to any competing claim. . . . Any nonabsolute value that is made absolute and demands to be the center of dedicated life is idolatry." From *Idolatry* (Cambridge, Mass.: Harvard University Press, 1992), pp. 245–246.

9. "When a finite value . . . [becomes] a *center of value* by which other values are judged . . . [and] has been elevated to centrality and imagined as a final source of meaning, then one has chosen what Jews and Christians call a *god*. . . . To be worshipped as a god, something must be sufficiently good to be plausibly regarded as the rightful center of one's valuing. . . . One has a god when a finite value is worshipped

Notes

and adored and viewed as that without which one cannot receive life joyfully." Thomas C. Oden, *Two Worlds: Notes on the Death of Modernity in America and Russia* (Downers Grove, Ill: InterVarsity Press, 1992), p. 95.

10. Margaret I. Cole, ed. *Beatrice Webb's Diaries, 1924–1932* (London: Longmans, Green, and Co., 1956), p. 65.

11. Brian Rosner does the best job of showing the basis for each of these three models in Biblical exegesis and the history of interpretation. See especially pp. 43–46 and Chapter 10 in Brian S. Rosner, *Greed as Idolatry: The Origin and Meaning of a Pauline Metaphor* (Grand Rapids, Mich.: Eerdmans, 2007). He bases much of his analysis on the work of Moshe Halbertal and Avishai Margalit, *Idolatry* (Cambridge, Mass.: Harvard University Press, 1992). Most books on idolatry tend to stress only one of the three models.

12. Biblical texts that spell out idolatry as adultery toward God as our true Spouse: Jeremiah 2:1–4:4; Ezekiel 16:1–63; Hosea 1–4; Isaiah 54:5–8; 62:5. See also Chapter 1, "Idolatry and Betrayal," in Halbertal and Margalit, *Idolatry*.

13. Biblical texts that spell out idolatry as self-salvation, rejecting God as our true Savior, include those in which God asks his people: *"Where are the gods you have made for yourselves? Let them come and save you when you are in trouble"* (Jeremiah 2:28). Cf. also Judges 10:13–14, Isaiah 45:20, Deuteronomy 32:37–38. Also see 1 Samuel 15:23, where arrogant self-sufficiency is considered idolatry.

14. Biblical texts that spell out idolatry as spiritual treason, betraying our true King: 1 Samuel 8:6–8, 12:12; Judges 8:23. Romans 1:25–26 teaches that whatever we worship

Notes

and center our lives on we must "serve" and obey (Verse 25). Verse 26 goes on to say this means that the heart falls into the grip of overwhelming, inordinate drives and desires. In the rest of the New Testament, these idolatrous, enslaving desires (Greek *epithumia*) are mentioned whenever the need for personal change is addressed. See Galatians 5:16ff; Ephesians 2:3, 4:22; 1 Peter 2:11, 4:2; 1 John 2:16; James 1:14ff. See also Chapter 8, "Idolatry and Political Authority," in Halbertal and Margalit, *Idolatry*.

15. Rebecca Pippert, *Out of the Saltshaker* (Downers Grove, Ill.: InterVarsity Press, 1979), p. 53.

16. The suicide was described in the blog post cited earlier at http://copycateffect.blogspot.com/2009/04/recess-x.html.

17. I have changed his name and the names of others throughout the book whose lives I use as examples of the principles we are treating.

ONE—All You've Ever Wanted

18. Cynthia Heimel, *If You Can't Live Without Me, Why Aren't You Dead Yet?* (New York: Grove Press, 2002), p. 13. This quote originally appeared in *The Village Voice*.

19. Halbertal and Margalit, *Idolatry*, p. 10.

20. Ishmael, though older, was born not of Abraham's wife, but of his wife's servant woman. Had Isaac not been born to Sarah, Ishmael would have been Abraham's heir.

21. Jon Levenson, *The Death and Resurrection of the Beloved Son: The Transformation of Child Sacrifice in Judaism and Christianity* (New Haven: Yale University Press, 1995).

Notes

22. For this rendering of Job 23:10, see Francis I. Anderson, *Job: An Introduction and Commentary* (Downers Grove, Ill.: InterVarsity Press, 1976), p. 230.

23. See 2 Chronicles 3:1. "Moriah" is a name given to the mountains and hills surrounding Jerusalem. On one of these hills, Jesus Christ was put to death.

24. Romans 3:26.

TWO—Love Is Not All You Need

25. Robert Alter, *Genesis: Translation and Commentary* (New York: W. W. Norton, 1996), pp. 151–157.

26. Ernest Becker, *The Denial of Death* (New York: Free Press, 1973), p. 160.

27. Ernest Becker, *The Denial of Death*, p. 167.

28. There has been a wave of articles and books on this minor cultural shift. See the article by Barbara F. Meltz, "Hooking Up Is the Rage, but Is It Healthy?" in *The Boston Globe*, February 13, 2007. Also see Laura Sessions Stepp, *Unhooked: How Young Women Pursue Sex, Delay Love, and Lose at Both* (New York: Riverhead, 2007).

29. *Mere Christianity*, Book II, Chapter 5, "Sexual Morality."

30. Why didn't Jacob simply refuse to go along with this bold, obvious swindle? Again, Robert Alter's insights are invaluable. When Jacob asks, "Why have you *deceived* me?" the Hebrew word is the same one used in chapter 27 to describe what Jacob did to Isaac. Alter then quotes an ancient rabbinical commentator who imagines the conversation the next day between Jacob and Leah. Jacob says to

Leah: "I called out 'Rachel' in the dark and you answered. Why did you do that to me?" And Leah says to him, "Your father called out 'Esau' in the dark and you answered. Why did you do that to him?" His fury dies on his lips. He sees what it is like to be manipulated and deceived, and he meekly complies with Laban's offer.

31. It is likely that, since most marriages were arranged in this way, many women felt unwanted by their husbands, and so this story would have had direct resonance to many readers in ancient times. If a modern reader finds offensive the whole account of women being bought and sold by men, it would be important to keep in mind that the overall thrust of the Genesis narrative is to undermine the practice by describing it so negatively. Robert Alter, in *The Art of Biblical Narrative,* says that if you read the book of Genesis and think it is condoning primogeniture, polygamy, and bride purchase, you are misunderstanding it. Throughout the book polygamy always wreaks devastation. It never works out. All you ever see is the misery the patriarchal institutions cause in families. Alter concludes that all the stories in Genesis are *subversive* to those ancient patriarchal practices.

32. Most English translations provide footnotes to tell you what the names mean. Leah gave birth to her first child, a boy, and she named him Reuben. Reuben meant "to see," for she thought, "Now maybe my husband will see me; I won't be invisible to him anymore." It did not happen. She then had a second son, and she named him Simeon, which had to do with hearing: "Now maybe my husband

will finally listen to me." Again he did not. She then had a third son and named him Levi, which meant "to be attached," and she said, "Finally, now that I've borne him *three* sons, my husband's heart will be attached to me."

33. Derek Kidner, *Genesis: An Introduction and Commentary* (Downers Grove, Ill.: InterVarsity Press, 1967), p.160.

34. C. S. Lewis, *Mere Christianity* (various editions), Book III, Chapter 10, "Hope."

35. C. S. Lewis, *Mere Christianity*, "Hope."

36. Ernest Becker, *The Denial of Death*, pp. 166–67.

37. Whatever happened, Dargis asks, to *Thelma and Louise*, the 1991 movie in which women "wore old blue jeans and confidently put the moves on men . . . and no marriage plans?" Manohla Dargis, "Young Women Forever Stuck at Square One in the Dating Game," *New York Times*, February 6, 2009.

38. Thomas Chalmers, "The Expulsive Power of a New Affection." This is a classic sermon by a nineteenth-century Scottish Presbyterian minister and statesman. The sermon is available many places on the Internet.

39. George Herbert, "Dulness" in *The Complete English Poems* ed. James Tobin (London: Penguin, 1991), p. 107.

THREE—Money Changes Everything

40. This account is taken from Jonathan Weber, "Greed, Bankruptcy, and the Super Rich" on the *Atlantic Monthly*'s Web site "Atlantic Unbound." Accessed May 30, 2009 at http://www.theatlantic.com/doc/200905u/yellowstone-club

Notes

41. Paul Krugman, "For Richer," *New York Times Magazine*, October 20, 2002. Krugman quotes John Kenneth Galbraith's 1967 book, *The New Industrial State:* "Management does not go out ruthlessly to reward itself—a sound management is expected to exercise restraint. . . . With the power of decision goes opportunity for making money. . . . Were everyone to seek to do so . . . the corporation would be a chaos of competitive avarice. But these are not the sort of thing that a good company man does; a remarkably effective code bans such behavior. Group decision-making insures, moreover, that almost everyone's actions and even thoughts are known to others. This acts to enforce the code and, more than incidentally, a high standard of personal honesty as well."

42. Friedrich Nietzsche, *The Dawn of Day*, trans. J. M. Kennedy (London: Allen and Unwin, 1911), pp. 209–210.

43. See the 2008 study from the Pew Research Center. Twenty-five percent of people called themselves "Lower" or "Lower-middle" class, 72 percent called themselves "Middle" or "Upper-Middle" class, and only 2 percent named themselves members of the "Upper Class." The report was accessed at http://pewresearch.org/pubs/793/inside-the-middle-class on July 1, 2009.

44. There is far more material in Luke-Acts about the relationship of the gospel to greed and idolatry than we can treat here. According to Luke, acquisitiveness is a sign of those who reject the call to follow Jesus, whether it is Judas (Acts 1:17–20), Ananias and Sapphira (5:1–11), or Simon the Sorcerer (8:18–24). Most telling of all, there are two

riots against Christians described in the Book of Acts, and in both cases, opposition to the gospel was motivated by greed (Acts 16:19–24; 19:23–41). The riot in Ephesus in Acts 19 is particularly instructive. Christianity was spreading and causing people to turn from idols. That affected the economy, since the banking system and the idol makers and shrines were all intertwined. Christianity changed the way people spent and used their money, and that threatened the cultural status quo.

45. See especially Chapters 9 and 10 in Brian S. Rosner, *Greed As Idolatry: The Origin and Meaning of a Biblical Metaphor* (Grand Rapids, Mich.: Eerdmans, 2007).

46. Richard Keyes speaks of "near" and "far" idols in "The Idol Factory," in *No God but God: Breaking with the Idols of Our Age* (Chicago: Moody, 1992), pp. 29ff. Here I sketch out a similar concept, but he defines "far idols" more as cognitive false belief systems, and in this chapter I speak of "deep idols" as motivational drives.

47. Joseph Frazier Wall, *Andrew Carnegie* (Pittsburgh: University of Pittsburgh Press, 1989), pp. 224–225. Quoted in the chapter "Andrew Carnegie," *The Wise Art of Giving: Private Generosity and the Good Society* (Maclean, Va: Trinity Forum, 1996), pp. 5–25.

48. "Andrew Carnegie," *The Wise Art of Giving*, pp. 5–26.

49. Annie Dillard, *An American Childhood,* quoted in *The Wise Art of Giving,* pp. 3–48.

50. The Bible sees idols not only as false lovers and pseudo-saviors, but as slave masters. The Bible understands all relationships with rulers, both divine and human, to be

covenantal in nature. People enter into a covenant or contract with their ruler and with their God. Both they and their ruler are bound by oath to fulfill the duties outlined in the covenant. To each covenant, blessings and curses are attached (see the end of the book of Deuteronomy). The covenant keeper gets specified blessings, while the covenant breaker receives the curses. If, then, a man centers his life on making a lot of money he has (unwittingly) entered into an idol covenant with moneymaking. This means money becomes his slave master. It will drive him to overwork, and to cut corners ethically in order to make money. And if his career falters he will find himself with a deep sense of failure and guilt that he cannot remedy. The reason is that his idol is "cursing" him. Since he has failed his ultimate "Lord," he cannot escape a sense of complete worthlessness. Unless he gets a new center for his life and a new "lord," he cannot escape the sense of being cursed.

FOUR—The Seduction of Success

51. Lynn Hirshberg, "The Misfit," *Vanity Fair,* April 1991, Volume 54, Issue 4, pp. 160–169, 196–202.

52. The actor Ben Cross, playing the 1924 Gold Medalist Harold Abrahams, speaks these words in the film. It would not be fair to attribute these motives to Harold Abrahams himself. But the writer of the screenplay has perfectly depicted the interior life of many success-oriented, ambitious people.

Notes

53. Article accessed on March 28, 2009, at http:/www.contact music.com/new/xmlfeed.nsf/mndwebpages/pollack moviesjustifymyexistence.

54. From "Success and Excess" by Harriet Rubin. This is the online edition that can be accessed at http://www.fast company.com/node/35583/print on March 28, 2009.

55. See the book-length study on this subject. Edward P. Meadors, *Idolatry and the Hardening of the Heart* (London and New York: T and T Clark, 2006).

56. *Good Housekeeping,* October 1990, pp. 87–88.

57. Peter L. Berger, Brigitte Berger, Hansfield Kellner, *The Homeless Mind: Modernization and Consciousness* (New York: Penguin, 1974), p. 89.

58. The David Brooks and Christopher Lasch quotes are taken from Nathan O. Hatch, "Renewing the Wellsprings of Responsibility," an address to the Council of Independent Colleges in Indianapolis, March 12, 2009.

59. Nathan O. Hatch, "Renewing the Wellsprings of Responsibility."

60. For more development of this argument see Timothy Keller, *The Reason for God* (New York: Dutton, 2007), the chapter on "The Cross."

61. We should not infer from this story of a slave girl forgiving her master that we should submit passively to oppression and injustice. The Bible's call to forgive *and* to seek justice are not mutually exclusive but complementary. Miroslave Volf, in his volumes *Exclusion and Embrace* (Nashville: Abingdon, 1996) and *The End of Memory: Remembering Rightly in a Violent World* (Grand Rapids, Mich.: Eerd-

mans, 2006) makes a strong case that it is necessary to forgive oppressors in order to truly seek justice. If you cannot do the interior work of forgiveness, you will seek excessive personal revenge rather than true justice, and so, ironically, you will remain oppressed. You will be drawn into the endless cycle of violent repayments yourself. Even in relationships that are not physically violent, but just unfair, you will not do a good job at confronting and correcting wrongdoers unless you first forgive them in your heart. If you don't forgive the perpetrator, you will overreach in your confrontation. You will be seeking not justice or change but only to inflict pain. Your demands will be excessive and your attitude abusive. The wrongdoer will see the confrontation as intended simply to cause hurt. A cycle of retaliation will begin. Only when you have lost the inner need to see the other person hurt will you have any chance of actually bringing about justice, change, and healing.

62. This is from the opening paragraph of "Success Excess" by Harriet Rubin. This is from the newsstand edition of *Fast Company*, October 1998. Current versions of this article now online have been revised.

63. This is a summary of a paragraph from the famous sermon by nineteenth-century Scottish minister Thomas Chalmers, "The Expulsive Power of New Affection" (available many places on the Internet). The paragraph itself reads: "It is thus that the boy ceases, at length, to be the slave of his appetite; but it is because a manlier taste has now brought it into subordination, and that the youth ceases to idolize

pleasure, but it is because the idol of wealth has become the stronger and gotten the ascendancy, and that even the love of money ceases to have the mastery over the heart of many a thriving citizen; but it is because, drawn into the whirl of city polities, another affection has been wrought into his moral system, and he is now lorded over by the love of power. There is not one of these transformations in which the heart is left without an object. Its desire for one particular object may be conquered; but as to its desire for having some one object or other, this is unconquerable."

FIVE—The Power and the Glory

64. Quoted in Bob Goudzwaard, *Idols of our Time* (Downers Grove, Ill: InterVarsity Press, 1984), p. 9.

65. From Robespierre's full speech quoted in Richard Bienvenu, *The Ninth of Thermidor* (Oxford: Oxford University Press, 1970), pp. 32–49.

66. Al Wolters, Michael Goheen, *Creation Regained: Basics for a Reformational Worldview,* second edition (Grand Rapids, Mich.: Eerdmans, 2005), p. 61.

67. "The lust for power is prompted by a darkly conscious realization of its insecurity." Reinhold Niebuhr, *The Nature and Destiny of Man: Volume I, Human Nature* (New York: Scribner, 1964), p. 189.

68. "The most obvious forms of idolatry are those in which the world of meaning is organized around a center . . . such as the life of a tribe or nation, which is patently contingent and not ultimate." Niebuhr, p. 165.

69. Goudzwaard, p. 23.

70. "Her [Germany's] boundless contemporary self-assertion which literally transgresses all bounds previously known in religion, culture, and law, is a very accentuated form of the power impulse. . . ." Niebuhr, p.189n.

71. C. S. Lewis, *Mere Christianity* (New York: HarperCollins, 2001), p. 11.

72. ". . . the effort is made to comprehend the meaning of the world through the principle of natural causation alone . . . [this] implies the deification of reason. That such an iden-tification represents idolatry and that the laws of reason and logic are incapable of fully comprehending the total meaning of the world, is attested by the fact that life and history are full of contradictions which cannot be resolved in terms of rational principles." Niebuhr, p. 165.

73. C. E. M. Joad, *The Recovery of Belief* (London: Faber and Faber, 1952), pp. 62–63.

74. Richard Crossman, ed., *The God that Failed* (New York: Harper, 1949).

75. See the interesting study by Steward Davenport, *Friends of the Unrighteous Mammon: Northern Christians and Market Capitalism 1815–1860* (Chicago: University of Chicago, 2008). Davenport tries to discover why some Christian leaders embraced Adam Smith's version of capi-talism, when it was clearly "ideological," asserting that if a government's only concerns were economic ones, morality and community would flourish naturally.

76. One thoughtful voice that has exposed the ideological na-ture of modern capitalism has been Wendell Berry, who

calls Americans to "waste less, spend less, use less, want less, need less." See his *Sex, Economy, Freedom, and Community: Eight Essays* (New York: Pantheon, 1994). Berry is not really liberal, since he is against big government, nor conservative or libertarian, since he balances individual rights against the common good more than conservatives would do. This makes his thought a good hedge against the development of modern ideologies.

77. Stephen Marglin, *The Dismal Science: How Thinking Like an Economist Undermines Community* (Cambridge: Harvard University Press, 2008). Marglin's point is that modern economics have become ideological, conceiving human beings as interest-maximizing individuals who don't need human community, who define themselves in terms of how much they can afford to consume, not their roles in a complex of human relationships. Over the last four centuries, this economic ideology has become the dominant ideology in much of the world.

78. Richard A. Posner, *A Failure of Capitalism: The Crisis of '08 and the Descent into Depression* (Cambridge: Harvard University Press, 2009). Posner makes the case against a major part of capitalist dogma, namely, that markets are self-correcting.

79. See William T. Cavanaugh, *Being Consumed: Economics and Christian Desire* (Grand Rapids, Mich.: Eerdmans, 2008). Cavanaugh discusses the temptation for Christians to seal off their private from their public lives in a society dominated by market capitalism. Traditionally, greed is one of the Seven Deadly Sins, and somehow we are supposed to avoid

it in our private life while pursuing it in our public, business life. Also, in our society we are called to define ourselves by what we consume, but in Christianity we are called to define ourselves by what we love. The logic and values of the market, Cavanaugh says, are spreading over into every area of life. This is because modern capitalism is "ideological."

80. Larry Elliott and Dan Atkinson, *The Gods that Failed: How Blind Faith in Markets Has Cost Us Our Future* (New York: Nation Books, 2009).

81. Niebuhr defined idolatry as raising some finite and relative thing to being "the final and ultimate value." Niebuhr, p. 225.

82. Roy Clements, *Faithful Living in an Unfaithful World* (Downers Grove, Ill: InterVarsity Press, 1998), p.153.

83. Reinhold Niebuhr, *The Nature and Destiny of Man: Volume I Human Nature* (New York: Scribner, 1964), p. 189.

84. Diana R. Henriques, "Madoff, Apologizing, Is Given 150 Years," *New York Times*, June 30, 2009.

85. "Bernard Madoff Gets 150 Years in Jail for Epic Fraud," Bloomberg News, June 29, 2009, http://www.bloomberg .com/apps/news?pid=20601087&sid=aHSYu2UPYrfo

86. Niebuhr, pp. 179–180.

87. *Ibid.*

88. What I am describing in this paragraph is how "surface idols"—sex, religion, money—can serve the "deep idol" of power. Compare this with what was said about deep and surface idols in Chapter Three.

89. Over the years many interpreters have worked to identify

every part of the idol as a historical kingdom. Since Nebuchadnezzar is said to be "the head" (Verses 36–39), it has been reasoned that each of the other metal parts of the idol must be the next dominant world power. But the dream probably cannot be interpreted so specifically. Notice that in Verse 35 we are told that the stone (the kingdom of God) breaks the whole idol to pieces *"at the same time."* If the kingdoms are centuries apart, how could the stone smash them all at the same time? I think that therefore the statue represents the world kingdoms in general, with all their might, and ways, and power. The dream is not giving us a specific sequence of specific kingdoms, nor is it emphasizing specific time frames. It is telling us that God is sovereign despite the rising of injustice and tyranny, and that all human power will be judged in the end. For a commentary that lays out this interpretive approach, see Tremper Longman, *The NIV Application Commentary: Daniel* (Grand Rapids, Mich.: Zondervan, 1999), pp. 79–93.

90. Christian Smith, *Soul Searching: The Religious and Spiritual Lives of American Teenagers* (Oxford: Oxford University Press, 2005), pp. 162–170.

91. Malcolm Gladwell, *Outliers* (New York: Little, Brown and Company: 2008), pp.125–128, 132–133, 156–158. Gladwell acknowledges that talent (heredity) and hard work are important to success, but he argues that environment is the biggest factor: including timing, family background, and culture.

92. For a book-length treatment on this theme, see Edward P. Meadors, *Idolatry and the Hardening of the Heart: A*

Notes

Study in Biblical Theology (London and New York: T and T Clark, 2006.)

93. C. S. Lewis, *The Chronicles of Narnia: The Voyage of the Dawn Treader* (New York: Harper Trophy, 2000), p. 91.

94. For a book-length treatment on this theme, see G. K. Beale, *We Become What We Worship: A Biblical Theology of Idolatry* (Downers Grove, Ill: InterVarsity Press, 2008).

95. Lewis, pp. 108–110.

six—The Hidden Idols in our Lives

96. Sheelah Kolhatkar, "Trading Down," *New York Times*, July 5, 2009.

97. The oath could be found online on June 10, 2009, at mbaoath.org/take-the-oath

98. "Forswearing Greed," in *The Economist*, June 6, 2009, p. 66. See also Leslie Wayne, "A Promise to Be Ethical in an Era of Immorality," in the *New York Times*, May 29, 2009.

99. Andrew Delbanco, *The Real American Dream: A Meditation on Hope* (Cambridge, Mass.: Harvard University Press, 1999), pp. 3, 23.

100. Delbanco, p. 5.

101. The "scoffer" (Hebrew *les*) is often translated "mocker" or "scorner." This figure appears fourteen times in the book of Proverbs. His problem is pride and arrogance (14:6, 21:24). See Bruce Waltke, *The Book of Proverbs: Chapters 1–15* (Grand Rapids, Mich.: Eerdmans, 2004), p. 114.

102. Among orthodox Christians, there are many people and churches that issue warnings against unbelief and error.

Indeed this often needs to be done, and Proverbs 26:28 says that a "flattering tongue," unwilling to criticize those in power, is destructive to the church. But many believers, even when they flag teaching and practices that should be flagged, do it with the characteristics of the scoffer in the book of Proverbs. In response to this charge, some of them point out that some biblical speakers and writers used sarcasm. That is true—you can see it in Elijah's debate with the prophets of Baal in 1 Kings 18, or especially in Paul's critique of his critics in 2 Corinthians 10–13. Sarcasm and irony can be effective ways to drive a point home, but derision and contempt cannot be the settled, main way that sinners talk to other sinners.

103. "Gifts of the Spirit are excellent things, but . . . they are not things which are inherent in the nature, as true grace and holiness are . . . gifts of the Spirit are, as it were, precious jewels, which a man carries about him. But true grace in the heart is, as it were, the preciousness of the heart, by which . . .the soul itself becomes a precious jewel. . . . The Spirit of God may produce effects on many things to which he does not communicate himself. So the Spirit of God moved on the face of the waters, but not so as to impart himself to the waters. But when the Spirit by his ordinary influences bestows saving grace, he therein imparts himself to the soul. . . . Yea, grace is as it were the holy nature of the Spirit of God imparted to the soul." From Jonathan Edwards, "Charity and Its Fruits, Sermon Two," in Paul Ramsey, ed., *Ethical Writings,* Volume 8 of *Works of Jonathan Edwards* (New Haven: Yale University Press, 1989), pp. 152–173.

Notes

104. See Timothy Keller, *The Prodigal God* (New York: Dutton, 2008).

105. Kenneth Gergen lists more than twenty psychological problems that have appeared only in the twentieth century with its new emphasis on self-fulfillment—anorexia, bulimia, stress, low self-esteem. See Kenneth Gergen, *The Saturated Self: Dilemmas of Identity in Contemporary Life* (Basic Books, 1991) p. 13.

106. The Bible passages quoted in this book are ordinarily taken from the New International Version. But in this chapter, I will rely on my own translation of the book of Jonah. (In this translation I depended most often on the insights of Jack Sasson, *Jonah: A New Translation with Introduction, Commentary, and Interpretation;* The Anchor Bible (New York: Doubleday, 1990); Phyllis Trible, *Rhetorical Criticism: Context, Method, and the Book of Jonah* (Minneapolis: Augsburg Fortress, 1994); and *Young's Literal Translation of the Bible*).

107. Leslie C. Allen posits that the memory of Jonah's blind nationalism would have been similar to the way we remember Hitler's assertion of the need for *Lebensraum*. Allen, *The Books of Joel, Obadiah, Jonah, and Micah* (Grand Rapids, Mich.: Eerdmans, 1976), p. 202. cf. Rosemary Nixon, *The Message of Jonah* (Downers Grove, Ill.: InterVarsity Press, 2003,), pp. 56–58). Both Nixon and Allen believe listeners would have remembered Jonah as a partisan and jingoist, and therefore would have been shocked to hear that he had been called to preach and spiritually warn people in the Assyrian capital of Nineveh.

108. Richard Lovelace, *The Dynamics of Spiritual Life* (Downers Grove, Ill.: InterVarsity Press, 1982), pp. 198, 212.

109. Jonathan Edwards in his work of moral philosophy, *The Nature of True Virtue*, argues that if you love your country more than God, you will be belligerent toward other nations and races. He points out that the Romans considered love of country to be the highest of all virtues, yet this priority "was employed as it were for the destruction of the rest of mankind." P. Ramsey, ed. *Ethical Writings*, in vol. 8 of *Works of Jonathan Edwards.*

110. Halbertal and Margalit give substantial treatment to this dynamic—namely, that idolatry stems from error and illusion in the mind, and errorneous beliefs lead in turn to idolatry. See chapters "Idolatry and Representation," "Idolatry as Error," "The Wrong God," and "The Ethics of Belief" in *Idolatry* (Cambridge: Harvard University Press, 1992).

111. Biblically, idolatry and mental error go hand in hand, and this helps us understand the relationship between the first commandment, "Have no other gods before me," and the second commandment, "Make no graven images." Not only are we forbidden to worship false gods, but we are not to try to make a visual image of the true God. Why would this be? Halbertal and Margalit explore this question at length and conclude that anyone who tries to produce images of God will lead him- or herself into distortions and reductions. For example, a picture might show God to be quite majestic but could it at the same time depict his great love? In the end, anyone trying to produce an image

of deity will create a distortion and therefore a false God, even if the intention is to worship the true God. One of the great areas of idolatry, then, is doctrinal or theological error. If a person believes in a God of love but not justice, or of holiness and not mercy, that person's understanding falls short of the biblical God and so he or she is actually an idolater, worshipping a false god. See Margalit and Halbertal, Chapters 2, 4, 5, and 6. The New Testament answer to the question why God forbids us making a physical likeness of him (Exodus 33:20) is that he himself has given us an image of himself—Jesus Christ, who is (literally) the *icon* of the invisible God (Colossians 1:15).

112. This paragraph summarizes Thomas Oden's *Two Worlds*, Chapter 6.

SEVEN—The End of Counterfeit Gods

113. David Clarkson, "Soul Idolatry Excludes Men from Heaven," in *The Practical Works of David Clarkson*, Volume II (Edinburgh: James Nichol, 1865), pp. 299ff.

114. Clarkson, p. 311.

EPILOGUE—Finding and Replacing Your Idols

115. On Romans 1:21–25, commentator Douglas Moo writes: "In . . . paradigmatic fashion, [Paul] describes the terrible proclivity of all people to corrupt the knowledge of God they possess by making gods of their own. The tragic process of 'god-making' continues apace in our own day. . . .

Thus, as verses 24–31 show, the whole dreadful panoply of sins that plague humanity has it roots in the soil of this idolatry." Douglas J. Moo, *The Epistle to the Romans* (Grand Rapids, Mich.: Eerdmans, 1996), p. 110.

116. "All those who do not at all times trust God and do not in all their works or sufferings, life and death, trust in His favor, grace and good-will, but seek His favor in other things or in themselves, do not keep this [First] Commandment, and practice real idolatry, even if they were to do the works of all the other Commandments, and in addition had all the prayers, obedience, patience, and chastity of all the saints combined. For the chief work is not present, without which all the others are nothing but mere sham, show, and pretense, with nothing back of them. . . . If we doubt or do not believe that God is gracious to us and is pleased with us, or if we presumptuously expect to please Him only through and after our works, then it is all pure deception, outwardly honoring God, but inwardly setting up self as a false [savior]. . . ." Excerpts from Martin Luther, *Treatise Concerning Good Works* (1520), Parts X, XI.

117. Luther was not the only great theologian to see that idolatry lay behind all sin. Saint Augustine wrote, "Sins are committed when, out of an immoderate litany for . . . the least goods, we desert the best and highest goods which are you, O Lord our God, and your truth and law." John K. Ryan, ed., *The Confessions of St. Augustine* (Doubleday, 1960) p. 71. See also John Calvin, *Institutes of the Christian Religion*, ed. J. T. McNeil (Westminster, 1961) I. II. 8 and 3.3.12. Also, Jonathan Edwards' great work on ethics, *The*

Nature of True Virtue, assumes that idolatry, a failure to love God supremely, is at the root of human failure to live virtuous lives.

118. M. Halbertal and A. Margalit, *Idolatry* (Cambridge, Mass.: Harvard, 1992), p. 6: "[Communally] shared values, derived from the association of fixed visual perceptions, create a certain shared sensibility in people. . . . The commandment 'You shall not follow their practices,' which is meant as a rejection of the lifestyle of the idolatrous culture, reflects a complex weave of lifestyle, ritual, and faith. . . . the category of idolatry includes a criticism of the culture in which idolatry developed."

119. Here is a brief list of idol categories. The list may help us see the broad scope of idolatry in order to better recognize our own:

Theological idols—Doctrinal errors that produce such distorted views of God that we end up worshipping a false god.

Sexual idols—Addictions such as pornography and fetishisms that promise but don't deliver a sense of intimacy and acceptance; ideals of physical beauty in yourself and/or your partner; romantic idealism.

Magic/ritual idols—Witchcraft and the occult. All idolatry is in the end a form of magic that seeks to rebel against the order of transcendent reality rather than submitting to it in love and wisdom.

Political/economic idols—Ideologies of the left, right, and libertarian that absolutize some aspect of political order and make it *the* solution. Deifying or demonizing free markets, for example.

Racial/national idols—Racism, militarism, nationalism, or ethnic pride that turns bitter or oppressive.

Relational idols—Dysfunctional family systems of codependency; "fatal attractions"; living your life through your children.

Religious idols—Moralism and legalism; idolatry of success and gifts; religion as a pretext for abuse of power.

Philosophical idols—Systems of thought that make some created thing the problem with life (instead of sin) and some human product or enterprise the solution to our problems (instead of God's grace).

Cultural idols—Radical individualism, as in the West, that makes an idol out of individual happiness at the expense of community; shame cultures that make an idol out of family and clan at the expense of individual rights.

Deep idols—Motivational drives and temperaments made into absolutes: a. Power idolatry: "Life only has meaning /I only have worth if—I have power and influence over others." b. Approval idolatry: "Life only has meaning /I only have worth if—I am loved and respected by _____." c. Comfort idolatry: "Life only has meaning /I only have worth if—I have this kind of pleasure experience, a particular quality of life." d. Control idolatry: "Life only has meaning /I only have worth if—I am able to get mastery over my life in the area of _____."

120. This saying is widely attributed to the archbishop, but I

have not been able to confirm it or identify a source. It may be a paraphrase.

121. According to the Bible, all idol worshippers look to counterfeit gods in order to get more freedom and control, but in the end the result is less freedom and control, a form of slavery. We think that by pursuing sex, money, and power rather than the true God we are striking a blow for liberation, but ultimately we become enslaved to these things. Using the marital metaphor for idolatry, Jeremiah 2 and Ezekiel 16 show that when we leave our True Spouse for other lovers, we fall into a kind of spiritual sexual addiction. "You said, 'It's no use! I love foreign gods, and I must run after them!'" (Jeremiah 2:25) "Indeed, on every high hill and under ever spreading tree you lay down as a prostitute" (Jeremiah 2:20).

122. David Powlison, "Idols of the Heart and Vanity Fair," *The Journal of Biblical Counseling,* Volume 13, Number 2 (Winter 1995).

123. A good place to begin would be Kenneth Boa, *Conformed to His Image* (Grand Rapids, Mich.: Zondervan, 2001). An important book to read as an introduction to spiritual disciplines is Edmund P. Clowney, *CM: Christian Meditation* (Vancouver, B.C.: Regent, 1979). Clowney makes important distinctions between the meditation techniques of Eastern mysticism and those of orthodox Christianity.

124. John Newton, *Works of John Newton,* Volume VI (Edinburgh, UK, and Carlisle, Pa.: Banner of Truth reprint), p. 45.

BIBLIOGRAPHY

Barton, Stephen C., ed. *Idolatry: False Worship in the Bible, Early Judaism, and Christianity.* London and New York: T and T Clark, 2007.

Beale, G. K. *We Become What We Worship: A Biblical Theology of Idolatry.* Downers Grove, Ill.: InterVarsity Press, 2008.

Benson, Bruce Ellis. *Graven Ideologies: Nietzsche, Derrida, and Marion on Modern Idolatry.* Downers Grove, Ill.: InterVarsity Press, 2002.

Bobick, Michael W. *From Slavery to Sonship: A Biblical Psychology for Pastoral Counseling.* Unpublished D. Min. dissertation, Westminster Theological Seminary, 1989.

Clarkson, David. "Soul Idolatry Excludes Men from Heaven," in *The Practical Works of David Clarkson,* Volume II. Edinburgh: James Nichol, 1865, pp. 299ff.

Goudzwaard, Bob. *Idols of Our Time.* Sioux City, Iowa.: Dordt College Press, 1989.

Halbertal, Moshe and Avishai Margalit, *Idolatry.* Cambridge, Mass.: Harvard University Press, 1992.

Bibliography

Keyes, Richard. "The Idol Factory," in Os Guinness and John Seel, eds., *No God But God: Breaking with the Idols of Our Age*. Chicago: Moody Press, 1992.

Lints, Richard. "Imaging and Idolatry: The Sociality of Personhood in the Canon," in Lints, Michael Horton, and Mark Talbot, eds., *Personal Identity in Theological Perspective*. Grand Rapids, Mich.: Eerdmans, 2006.

Luther, Martin. *Larger Catechism* with study questions by F. Samuel Janzow. Saint Louis: Concordia, 1978.

Meadors, Edward P. *Idolatry and the Hardening of the Heart: A Study in Biblical Theology*. London and New York: T and T Clark, 2006.

Niebuhr, Reinhold. "Man as Sinner," in *The Nature and Destiny of Man*, Volume 1, Human Nature. New York: Scribner, 1964.

Nietzsche, Friedrich. *The Twilight of the Idols* and *The Anti-Christ*, translated by R. J. Hollingdale. New York: Penguin, 1990.

Oden, Thomas C. *Two Worlds: Notes on the Death of Modernity in America and Russia*. Downers Grove, Ill.: InterVarsity Press, 1992.

Oden, Thomas C. "No Other Gods" in Carl Braaten, Christopher Seitz, eds., *I Am The Lord Your God: Christian Reflections on the Ten Commandments*. Grand Rapids, Mich.: Eerdmans, 2005.

Powlison, David. "Idols of the Heart and Vanity Fair." *The Journal of Biblical Counseling*, Volume 13, Number 2, Winter 1995.

Bibliography

This article has been in circulation for over two decades and has been seminal for my thinking. It is also online at http://www.ccef.org/idols-heart-and-vanity-fair.

Ramachandra, Vinoth. *Gods That Fail: Modern Idolatry and Christian Mission*. Downers Grove, Ill.: InterVarsity Press, 1996.

Rosner, Brian S. *Greed as Idolatry: The Origin and Meaning of a Pauline Metaphor.* Grand Rapids, Mich.: Eerdmans, 2007.

Westphal, Merold. *Suspicion and Faith: The Religious Uses of Modern Atheism*. The Bronx, N.Y.: Fordham University Press, 1999.

ACKNOWLEDGMENTS

Again I thank Jill Lamar, David McCormick, and Brian Tart, my literary dream team that keeps stimulating and encouraging me in my writing. Also, thanks to Janice Worth and Lynn Land, who help me get away to write each summer.

This book is about our culture, and at my age people often lose their sympathy for it, and therefore their understanding of it. I have been fortunate in my sons—David, Michael, and Jonathan—in more ways than I can number. The one that bears most directly on this book is their wise, clear-eyed observation of the idols of their worlds, and their willingness to talk to me about them, long and intensely. Guys, thanks for the walks, dinners, and just hanging out. I respect how you've grown up loving the city and have become men of integrity.

I want to thank Kathy, who labored with me over

the book for months and over the ideas behind the book for years. I must say to Kathy what John Newton wrote to his wife Polly, namely, it is no wonder if so many years, so many endearments, so many obligations have produced such an uncommon effect, that by long habit, it is almost impossible for me to draw a breath, in which you are not involved.

About the Author

TIMOTHY KELLER was born and raised in Pennsylvania, and educated at Bucknell University, Gordon-Conwell Theological Seminary, and Westminster Theological Seminary. He was first a pastor in Hopewell, Virginia. In 1989 he started Redeemer Presbyterian Church in Manhattan, with his wife, Kathy, and their three sons. Today Redeemer has more than 5,000 regular Sunday attendees, plus the members of more than 100 new churches around the world. Also the author of *The Prodigal God* and the *New York Times* bestseller *The Reason for God*, he lives in New York with his family.